DATE DUE

Taming the Tokolosh

Through Fear into Healing
A Trauma Survivor's True Story

Taming the Tokolosh

Through Fear into Healing
A Trauma Survivor's True Story

by

Mandy Bass

New York, New York

Published by MidTown Publishing Inc.
1001 Avenue of Americas
12th Floor
New York, NY 10018

Library of Congress Control Number: 2017917228

ISBN 978-1-62677-018-8 (print book)
ISBN 978-1-62677-019-5 (eBook)
ISBN 978-1-62677-020-1 (audiobook)

Contents

Dedication

This book is dedicated to those of us who are great at helping others—but often forget to care for ourselves. I am deeply grateful to the friends, clients and family members who supported me during difficult times. And also to my editor, Angela Kelsey, who made this book possible from the beginning when she asked, "What if this experience turned out to be the best thing that ever happened to you?" and in the end helped me turn my story into a good read. This book is as much hers as mine.

Please read these disclaimers:

This is a true story based on my memory of events. All persons are real people; there are no composite characters. Occasionally, dialogue consistent with the character or nature of the person speaking has been supplemented. The names of some individuals have been changed to respect their privacy.

Nothing in this book is intended to diagnose or treat any condition of the mind or body. The mind tools, therapies and healing techniques described are intended for informational purposes only and should not be considered a substitute for medical care, professional counseling or psychotherapy.

Though I am currently a member of a Zen group, my spiritual beliefs are universal, eclectic and deeply personal. I have tried to give context to the spiritual exercises and concepts I share here. They should not be judged as belonging to any one religion or spiritual tradition. I have no desire—and make no attempt—to change anyone's mind about their religious beliefs. I share these ideas simply because they were beneficial to my healing process. Much research now supports the fact that meditation, compassion and Positive Psychology speed the healing process, and that research also shows that we can build new neuro-pathways in our brains that facilitate positive change.

Taming the Tokolosh

**Through Fear into Healing
A Trauma Survivor's True Story**

Part 1: The Assault

The Attack

I lay in fetal position on the cold floor of my family room as a drop of blood mingled with the rosy flecks in the beige tile flooring. I was too afraid to move. Then darkness welcomed me in and I drifted into the warm comfort of unconsciousness.

The urgent voice in my head was insistent: *Get up! If you don't find a way to get out now, he is going to kill you and no one will ever know what happened.*

Frozen in pain and fear, I tried to make sense of what was happening. I was certain I was going to die.

The wild-eyed intruder kicked me in the ribs.

"Do you believe in the forgiveness of Jesus Christ?" he ranted. "Do you?"

He kicked me again.

What does he want me to say?

"Get up!" my inner voice urged.

I struggled desperately to get to my feet but the brutal beating I had taken from the six-feet-tall madman was too much for my five-feet-two-inch, 112-pound frame.

What was this crazy guy doing in my home on a Sunday afternoon? He was well-dressed and didn't look like a hoodlum. But there he was, towering over me in my sanctuary, unleashing his wild rage.

Why? I had no idea. I was certain I'd never seen him before.

I live in a quiet, safe, middle-income neighborhood in Melbourne—known to my friends as Mel-boring—Florida. It was Super Bowl Sunday.

As was my normal routine, I went to my weekly Zen meditation group in the morning, followed by grocery shopping. When I got home, I prepared a large pot of home-made chicken soup. While the soup simmered on the stove, I sat down at my desk and opened my email, determined to get a head start on the busy week ahead.

Then came the sound of crashing glass from the opposite side of the house. Had one of my cats knocked something over?

The sound of glass shattering reverberated through the house. My mind grasped for clues.

"Must be something big," I thought.

Finally, I concluded that the large mirror in my master bathroom had come unglued from the wall.

"Ugh, what a mess," I imagined, and continued typing. I was in no hurry to walk into a shower of broken glass.

I finished the email I was working on and got up to investigate. Unhurried, I walked across the living room, toward the master suite, the cleanup of glass my only concern.

Then I saw him. A tall, dark figure emerged from the

shadows between my bathroom and bedroom.

He saw me, too, and rushed toward me.

Not being much of a fighter, I applied the same strategy I use when my cat drags in a live rat: I screamed. It never worked for rats. It didn't work this time either.

"Get out!" I shouted, mustering up courage I didn't feel, pointing to the front door.

He was in my face now, less than a foot away. I was more confused than scared. Who was he? Slender and athletic, his young, black face looked soft and innocent, except for the craziness in his eyes. What was he doing in my home?

Mimicking me, he pointed at the door and yelled back, "Get out!"

Huh?

His fist smashed my face.

What the hell? How can this be happening to me?

Another blow.

Shooting stars pierced the blackness of my vision as my head hit the floor hard and I lost consciousness. For a moment, nothing but deep stillness. Then, as he kicked me repeatedly, I became aware of his shoe in my ribs and back. Remembering where I was, I curled into a ball to protect my organs and covered my head with my arms.

Mind whirling, I worried about my eighty-year-old mother. How would she manage? She depends on me for all her financial support, and even her bank account is under my name.

How would she manage with me dead? Would she remember

that I have life insurance?

What about my cats? Who would care for them? Would he hurt them too?

The kicking stopped. I lay motionless.

Does he think I'm dead? What will he do with my body?

A few moments passed in stillness. I was afraid to move or risk opening my eyes.

Then, from out of nowhere, the mood changed.

"I am so sorry! So sorry!" the attacker cried out suddenly, as if in shock at his own behavior.

Cautiously I glanced up at him, still shielding my head with my arms. He looked bewildered, like he was waking up from a bad dream.

Distraught, he offered his hand, bending over to help me up.

Relief washed over me. I was confused by the sudden shift, and hesitantly extended my hand to allow him to help me up. I struggled for balance on my wobbly legs.

"Thank God this is over!" I thought.

But it wasn't.

No sooner was I up than a dark cloud of rage came over him again. Next thing I knew, the madness was back. Before I could protect my face, his fist smashed into my mouth.

Teeth tearing through my bottom lip, I fell backward and heard my skull crack as I hit the floor.

As the blood trickled down my neck and I played dead on the floor again, I couldn't help but wonder why this insane situation was happening to me now.

"No time for that!" I told myself. I knew I had to get out or I was going to die.

Adrenalin pumping, I stumbled to my feet and made a mad dash for the front door.

My hands fumbled uncontrollably as I struggled to get the front door unlocked. Finally, it was open and I reached for the handle of the glass storm door on the other side.

Crap! It was locked too. Why? I never do that!

Too late.

I could feel him behind me now. He grabbed my arm and yanked me back into the dining room.

The door slammed shut and I was trapped again.

I swung around to see him holding a large heavy chair over his head. He lunged forward, aiming it at my head.

Instinctively, I blocked with my right arm.

Crack! Arm broken but head intact.

Thank God!

He lost his balance from the break in momentum, and stumbled and struggled to regain control of the heavy chair.

I ran for the door again. With numb fingers, I fumbled with the door handle, excruciating pain shooting through my arm. Somehow, I opened the front door and unlocked the storm door without looking back.

It was still daylight. I set my sites on the front door of the house across the street, praying that someone was at home, or that a neighbor would drive by and see what was happening.

Why hadn't I been more neighborly? Will they recognize me or think I am crazy? I must look like a bloody mess. I wish I knew their names.

I knew he could outrun me, but I was hopeful that someone would see us and come to my rescue, or at least call the police. Weak and in pain, I knew this was my last opportunity to make it out alive.

Escape

Breathing heavily, eyes focused on the house across the street, I made a mad dash over the lawn. I knew he would be right behind me and I was certain that he was a lot faster than I was.

Midway across the front yard, I was grabbed from the side. Focused straight ahead like a racehorse with blinders, I hadn't seen it coming.

Shit! Not again!

I turned to push the monster away, determined not to be dragged back inside again.

But this time when I turned to face my attacker, I was surprised. It wasn't the madman grabbing my arm at all, but a uniformed police officer, trying to pull me to safety.

Where did he come from?

My knees buckled and I collapsed on the ground.

"Get her away from the house!" another officer yelled.

What? Another one?

I looked up and down the street to see a swarm of police cars and officers in uniforms. *What the heck is going on?*

Legs weak, I sat down on the neighbor's lawn as soon

as the officer allowed.

Agonizing pain spread through my arm, wrist and fingers. My neck, back and face were wet with blood.

The street buzzed with activity.

What the hell are all these people doing out here?

The sky was an exquisite mosaic of vivid color—a glorious Florida sunset.

I took a deep breath and tasted the crisp, clean air.

Chilled to the bone, I shivered uncontrollably. A neighbor covered my shoulders with a warm jacket.

Finally, I was safe. Free.

Flashing lights, fire-rescue red, headed my way. Paramedics leapt out of their vehicle in a smooth, slow-motion symphony. The sky was alive in gold and blue. It was all so beautiful.

Pain radiated through my body like a crack skating across a frozen lake, but I didn't care. I was breathing in the magnificent tapestry in the sky, the calmness of the tall oak tree in my front yard and the gentle rustling of its leaves. Having escaped the clutches of a violent death, gratitude rushed through my veins. I felt high.

"How are you feeling?" the paramedic asked as he began to take my blood pressure.

"Great, thank you. How are you?" I said, as if greeting a neighbor on a morning walk. He looked at my swollen, bleeding face and shaking body.

"She is going into shock. Get the IV!" he shouted.

Shock? I couldn't recall the last time I was this happy

to be alive.

On the way to the hospital, the paramedics tended to my wounds. Safe in the emergency vehicle, I closed my eyes as my body began to unwind, and I drifted off, going back, way back, to my childhood home in South Africa.

Sobbing uncontrollably, I ran as fast as my little five-year-old legs would carry me, and burst into Mary's room. She was dressed in a starched green and white plaid apron with a matching head scarf.

The sparsely furnished bedroom smelled of paraffin oil used to light the lamp next to the bed.

"What is wrong, my darling?" she whispered, picking me up and holding me against her chest.

"Tell your nanny what's the matter." Cradling me in her soft black arms, Mary rocked back and forth and stroked the blond hairs on my forehead.

"When you go back home, can I come with you?" I asked.

"Ah, Miss Mandy you don't mean that."

"Yes, I do!"

"Why do you want to come with me and leave your family?" she asked gently.

"Because they hate me."

"I don't think that is true, Mandy, my darling."

"Yes, they do. They said so."

"Your sisters don't mean that. I tell you what, why don't we go in the house and I will pour you a nice glass of milk. Then we can play a game."

She put me down on a small, thin, shabby rug on the cement floor next to the bed.

"Mary, why is your bed so high? How do you get in at night?"

Immediately I crawled under the bed to investigate and discovered several bricks under each leg of the bed.

"Mary, why do you have your bed on bricks?"

"Let's go get you some milk," she said, changing the subject.

"No, I want to know! Why is your bed so high?"

"I'll tell you later."

"No, I want to know now."

"Let's go get you some milk."

She started walking out of the room.

"Come on!" she said, acting as if she would lock me in.

I ran out the door and into the courtyard that led to the main house, calling for my sisters.

I was the youngest of five girls, the much younger "surprise" baby, born after my parents had adopted my four sisters.

"Cheryl, Cheryl," I shouted to one of my sisters inside the house. "Mary's bed is on bricks. Come see!"

Excited to share what I had just discovered, I barged into the playroom, where three of my older sisters were intently practicing their version of "the twist" as Chubby Checker's "Let's Twist Again" blared from the record player.

The three of them were very close in age and interests. My mother liked to dress us all in the same outfits, like the Von Trapp family in *The Sound of Music*. But the three of them, who were in the beginning stages of adolescence, had had enough of that.

To my older sisters, I was a baby, a nuisance and a pest. Nine-year-old Cheryl, who looked like a doll, with dark brown hair and big, dark, sultry eyes, stopped dancing the second she saw me walk in the room. She crossed her arms defiantly and gave me a stare that said, "Get out!"

"You will never guess what I just saw." I could barely contain myself. "Mary sleeps on bricks."

"I told you to leave us alone!" shouted Adrienne, the pretty tomboy, with butterscotch-blond hair, a pixie nose, blue eyes and freckles. "We don't want you here."

"I came to tell you that Mary's bed is on a pile of bricks."

"No, it is not," said Cheryl, who was next to me in age and therefore disagreed with everything I said on principle.

"Yes, it is," I insisted.

"Yes, it is," Gail, the oldest of the three, agreed. She was eleven, tall, slender with chestnut-colored hair, brown eyes and a heart of gold. Since our oldest sister, Mary-Anne, had gone to boarding school, I counted on her to protect me from the other two sisters when needed.

Cheryl pouted and looked to Adrienne for support.

"Tsk! Don't you know anything?" Adrienne

said, putting her hands on her hips and pushing out her chest as Mary walked into the room. "That is because of the Tokolosh! Tell them, Mary. Tell them about the Tokolosh. That's why your bed is on bricks. You are afraid of the Tokolosh."

Mary's face turned grey. "I don't want to talk about it."

Adrienne began chanting: "Mary is afraid of the Tokolosh! Mary is afraid of the Tokolosh!"

"You be quiet! We will have no more of this talk!" Mary said in her sternest voice. She turned and walked out of the room.

"What is the Tokolosh, Adrienne?" I asked. "Tell me, tell me."

Gail looked worried and tried to intervene, saying, "I don't think this is a good idea. She is too young."

But it was too late. Adrienne took center stage, with the enviable role of pulling back the curtain on the scariest creature a five-year-old could dare to imagine.

Turning off the record player, blue eyes twinkling, she got up onto a chair, made a dramatic gesture with her arms, and took a bow. Then she stuck out her chest, paused for effect and began in a hushed tone:

"The Tokolosh is the scariest creature in the world, uglier than the ugliest monster you can imagine . . ."

She described his gouged-out eyes and scaly tail, explaining that he was an evil spirit who killed people—especially little children—and made them sick and took over their bodies.

"He can turn himself invisible just by drinking water," Adrienne elaborated, as if the killing of little children and taking over their bodies were not sufficiently terrifying.

"So, why does she have bricks under her bed?" asked Cheryl, who was also hearing about the Tokolosh for the first time.

"I think that is because the Tokolosh is short and can't climb so high," I suggested.

The paramedic's voice beamed me back across the fifty-year span instantly: "Okay, let's get you inside."

Opening my eyes, I saw the handsome face of the paramedic preparing my gurney as his partner opened the back door of the emergency van. We had arrived at the hospital.

He began to remove the blood-stained yellow blanket that was draped over the gurney.

"It is so cold," I said, starting to shiver again.

"You know what? Keep the blanket. After what you've been through, you deserve it."

"I bet you say that to all the pretty girls you pick up in this thing," I replied, feebly attempting a bit of humor.

Resuscitating the Psyche

B y the time a K9 unit was sent in to storm my house, and a German Shepherd subdued my attacker, I had racked up $11,000 in emergency charges at Holmes Regional Medical Center.

After being poked, prodded, cat-scanned and x-rayed, I was pronounced "stable," and made available to the police for interview. A uniformed officer came into the room, chatted with me briefly and then turned his attention to a laptop computer in the corner. A few minutes later he turned around and left abruptly.

My head was throbbing and the intensity of the fluorescent light made me nauseous. Everything was beginning to hurt.

After a while, the policeman returned with a younger officer, also in uniform. The two fumbled around a bit with the computer and another electronic gadget. Then one officer left the room and returned a few minutes later with a third officer. The three of them huddled in the corner around the frozen computer. In hushed tones, they talked back and forth about what to do next. Later I found out that it was their first week on the job.

"Try control, alt, delete," I advised, welcoming something—anything—to distract myself from the pain I was in.

The cops stared at me blankly. I've never seen Keystone Cops but I imagined them to be something like this.

Hyper-alert, I was propped up in a hospital bed. A nurse popped her head in to tell us that someone would be coming by shortly to give me a tetanus shot, staple my head and put a cast on my arm.

I had been at the hospital for hours already and was feeling edgy and impatient.

Why do they need a computer to take my statement? What about pen and paper?

Since it was Super Bowl Sunday, I imagined the more tenured officers, those who knew how to operate the equipment, at home, glued to their televisions, surrounded by friends, beer and buffalo wings.

Eventually, one of the young cops got a voice recorder working and started asking questions, the laptop silent and defiant in the corner.

"How many times did he hit you?" he asked.

Mentally I ran through what I could remember of the assault, trying to count the number of times he hit me so I could give an accurate answer.

"How many?" he demanded impatiently.

"Give me a moment. I am trying to count them. You made me lose my place. Now I'll have to start from the beginning. One . . . two . . ."

"Was it more than three?"

"Yes. Of course."

"Okay, we will say multiple. . ."

When the police interview was over, I asked, "Who called you? How did you know to come to my house?"

"We were responding to a domestic situation on Cornell Street," he replied.

"Cornell Street?" I asked. "That's at least a half-mile away, in a different neighborhood."

A physician came in and the officer left the room. He put my arm in a cast and said he was going to give me a shot of morphine.

"Oh, no thanks," I said to the physician. "I'd rather have some Tylenol."

"Are you sure? You've been through a lot. The pain is going to get much worse. The morphine will help you sleep."

I didn't want to sleep yet. The dream about the Tokolosh was playing in my mind. It felt like a warning of sorts, something I needed to get to the bottom of. I knew that the suddenness of the attack, combined with the brutal beating I had taken, made the probability of PTSD higher than I was comfortable sleeping on.

From years of teaching and practicing hypnosis, neuro-linguistic programming and other brain-related modalities, I had experience with effective techniques that help to release the mind from the grip of trauma. I had used some of these methods very successfully in my coaching practice to help people disassociate from traumatic memories that were keeping them stuck. I reasoned that if I could apply some of those techniques before I slept, it would be quicker and easier for my brain to "return to normalcy."

It hurt to talk, so I just said, "Tylenol is fine."

The policeman who had taken my statement came back in to pass along a message from the supervising officer who was running things at the crime scene. I tried to get more information about how the police were already outside my house when I managed to escape.

"It will all be in the police report, ma'am," he assured me before relaying the information he was instructed to give me: the attacker was now in custody; they had secured the broken window with a hurricane shutter and turned off the chicken soup. But my two cats, who I had been asking about, were nowhere to be found.

That worried me.

What happened to them? Perhaps they escaped through the open window and got lost. Maybe they cut themselves on the broken glass. It's hours past their mealtime now. They must be hungry and frightened. If the intruder didn't hurt them, what about the police dogs? They are terrified of dogs.

Two of my cats were killed by dogs a few years prior and I could feel panic rising to the surface.

"Stay calm," I said to myself. "Breathe! Focus on your breath. Nice, slow deep breaths. That's right."

I was also hyper-aware that the longer I stayed away

from the scene of the crime, the harder it would be for me to go back. Given that the crime scene was my business and my home, avoiding it didn't seem like a viable option.

"I want to go home," I said to the nurse. "Please!"

"You really should stay overnight," the nurse insisted. "Don't you have anyone I can call?"

I could think of at least two dozen friends who would drop whatever they were doing to help me out, but they all lived two hundred miles away.

I had relocated to the area the previous year, and because I am self-employed and work from home, I had not met many locals. Except for people I met at the Zen Center and the gym, I'd remained isolated and alone.

Now there was no one within a two-hour drive whom I would be comfortable calling for help, especially in the middle of the night.

I moved painfully. Seeing my discomfort, the nurse asked, "Are you sure you don't want a morphine shot?"

Once again, I declined. Given the terror I had just been through, I was afraid of what might happen if I allowed the mischief of morphine to have its way with my mind and imagination.

After much back and forth with the hospital staff about what was best for me, they grudgingly agreed to let me go home.

Home Alone

A young police officer drove me home as the last few minutes of the Super Bowl played out on a video console on the front seat and I sat silently by myself in the back.

The house was spooky and cold. Blood spots and shards of glass were strewn everywhere. After a quick walkthrough, the young cop left and I was alone in the eerie stillness.

I turned up the heat but the thirty-seven-degree draft from the broken bathroom window continued to chill the air. I shivered as the frightening reality of what had happened pierced my psyche.

Bruised and swollen, I hobbled around the house, realizing the difficulty of even the simplest tasks without the use of my right arm.

I called for the cats. No response. I could only imagine the trauma they had experienced when their safe house turned into a house of horror.

"Stop thinking like that!" I told myself. "Let's visualize them coming home safe and sound." I called, waited a while, then called again. Silence.

Leaning against the Frappuccino-colored sofa, I closed my eyes as I tried to relax my aching body and keep my negative thoughts at bay. I knew that no matter what the reality was, allowing my mind to conjure up bad scenarios of what could happen would not improve anything, and only make matters worse. Instead I created a picture in my mind of Sophia, my silky black cat with big hazel-green eyes, gracefully prancing through the cat door, just as she had done many times before. Next came charcoal grey Mako, not quite as graceful, but equally adored, meowing loudly, demanding he be fed right away. I imagined the relief and the happiness I would feel.

"Come home," I urged them. "Please, come home, safe."

Finally, I got my phone and propped myself up on the sofa, facing the cat door. Then I called my friend Lourdes. She picked up the phone right away.

I first met Lourdes when she attended one of my personal growth seminars in the late nineties, when I was an instructor of The Silva Mind Training Method and had a strong following in South Florida. In those days, I gave keynote talks across the country, and was privileged to share stages with Wayne Dyer, Deepak Chopra and Gregg Braden. The concepts and methodologies I taught, while widely accepted today, were considered quite radical then.

I had seen myself as a smuggler of ideas, sneaking innovative, and often eyebrow-raising methodologies into the business world. Realizing that labels were important for acceptance into corporate America, I taught meditation as "Energy Management," visualization as "Focus Management," Neuro-Linguistic Programming (NLP) as "The Art of Influence," and Emotional Intelligence Techniques as "Essential Sales Skills." That seemed like a long time ago.

Lourdes was a fervent learner and absorbed new ideas like a sponge. As an emotional wellness coach, she was highly skilled, super smart and naturally empathetic. She put what she learned to her own use immediately. Then she went on to do advanced training for the benefit of her clients.

Eventually I became her business coach, and we developed a strong mutual liking and trust.

A few years later when I went into an emotional tailspin over a relationship that had gone amok, I turned to her for help. After that crisis, our business relationship evolved into a deep friendship.

All in all, we had known each other for more than fifteen years. Even though it was the middle of the night, I knew I could call her.

Wrapped in the blood-stained, bright yellow paramedic's blanket, I lay on the couch, holding the phone to my ear with my left hand. My mummified right arm rested on a pile of pillows as I described the day's events to Lourdes.

Like a moth caught in a light fitting, my mind raced chaotically from one disassociated thought to another. Then it plunged into a swirling web of anxiety.

"What's happening now? What are you feeling?" Lourdes asked eventually, breaking the silence we had fallen into.

The question seemed almost overwhelming.

"Mandy," Lourdes said again, "tell me what's going on. What are you feeling?"

Feeling? Earlier I had been shifting back and forth between fear and gratitude, but now I felt nothing. Nothing at all.

"Nothing," I said, searching my mind for something tangible to focus on, something I could control. My attention ping-ponged between the crisis I was suddenly in, unanswered questions about the day's events, and irrelevant details of my "To-Do" list.

Finally, I had something I could grasp that I felt safe talking about, and asked, "Do you think I should cancel my launch?"

"What?" she asked incredulously.

"Remember we have that big launch planned for FreeSpeakerBureau.com? I have lots of affiliates lined up. I guess I should let them know tomorrow. I don't think we will be able to pull it off now. Do you?"

"I don't think you need to make that decision right now. How about tonight we just focus on making sure you are safe and taken care of?"

She suggested we take a few moments to process what had happened. We stopped talking and breathed together as the two hundred miles that separated us disappeared. She reminded me that the danger was over and I was now safe.

"I am going to find someone to watch Nicholas and I'll come get you," she said.

"No. Don't do that. There is no need for you to leave your son in the middle of the night and drive all the way up here."

"You can stay in Miami with me. Can you call your neighbor to come stay with you until I get there?" Lourdes asked.

"That isn't necessary. I am fine. Really. I don't want to be all the way down in Miami. I need to be home. I have a business to run. I'll call my mom in the morning and she can drive up then."

"Can you call her now?"

"Honestly, I am fine." I tried to reassure her.

"Why can't you call your mom now?"

"Lourdes, it's the middle of the night and my mother doesn't drive in the dark. No point calling her now and getting her all upset. I promise I will do it first thing in the morning."

I was hoping that it wouldn't be necessary. That I would wake up and realize the whole situation was a bad dream.

"I don't think you should be alone right now," she said again.

"I will be okay. I just want my cats to come home." The night outside the sliding glass door looked darker than ever before. Tears welled up as a veil of uncontrollable dread descended upon me. I kept telling myself to keep it real, not to blow things out of proportion.

"I am sure they didn't go far. They'll come home," she said.

I shivered, feeling the wind coming in through the broken window, imagining my cats out in the cold, lost and afraid.

"Yeah," I replied unconvincingly, trying to shake off the fear and gain a sense of control.

I tried to visualize the cats coming through the door again and bring back the relief and happiness I'd created forty minutes earlier, before I called Lourdes, but I couldn't quite get those feelings back.

"Are you okay?" Lourdes asked.

"Yes. I'm fine. Let's both try to get some sleep."

"Okay, but keep the phone next to you. If you need anything or you just want to talk, call me. I'll check in with you in a few hours."

After we hung up, I remembered that I wanted to use an NLP trauma technique before I went to sleep so I could desensitize the events of the day and maintain some degree of control.

One of the most effective ways to take a negative charge out of past events is to mentally play the event sequence backwards, as if you were watching a movie in rewind: to mentally see it going from the end, where you are safe, all the way back to the beginning, to a safe, happy scene, before the event happened.

Each time you repeat the process of going through the sequence backward, from an observer's perspective, it makes a remarkable difference in your neurology, and your mind changes its associations with the memory. After repeating the process a few times, most people find that they still have the memory of the experience completely accessible to them, but the negative charge disintegrates.

After a few unsuccessful tries to practice the technique on my own, I realized that I could not focus or concentrate long enough to do the exercise. My mind kept skipping to questions I could not answer.

What were the police doing outside my house? If they were chasing the attacker, they must have seen him break in. Why didn't they do something? Why didn't they help me? Why did he choose my house?

Eventually I remembered a CD I had created years earlier that included the NLP technique. I hobbled into my office to find the guided visualization exercise. I knew I had the MP3 on my computer.

When I walked into the room, I could feel the hairs on the back of my neck stand up. My computer was still on, my email open and everything was mostly as it had been when I stood up earlier in the day to investigate the sound of breaking glass. But my leather lounge chair was out of place and the ottoman was upside down.

"This is where the dogs got him!" I said out loud, looking around at the crime scene. Then I saw a pink Post-it note on the desk with a message from my attacker, written in blue Sharpie ink: **"Don't do LSD."**

I felt the edges of panic creeping into my psyche.

"Relax, Mandy," I told myself. "You are safe! Everything is okay now. He is locked up."

I sat down at my desk and clumsily toggled the mouse with my left hand, looking for the MP3 that would get me through the night.

After seeing the note from my attacker, and realizing he may have gone through my things, my office felt very creepy. I found the audio file, turned up the volume so I would be able to hear it in the family room, and hobbled back to the sofa, determined to practice the exercise. The audio included a deep relaxation exercise that soothed me into some much-needed sleep.

Dark Night

A sharp pain in my skull jolted me awake. It was 2:12 AM. Head pounding, I instinctively felt for the tender area on my scalp where the soreness was most intense. My hair was matted with dried blood, and I could feel the staples that had been used to close the gash over my left ear. My head felt like it was going to explode.

I remembered the cats.

Did they come in while I was asleep?

I moved to get up and go call for them again.

The throbbing in my head picked up its pace and I could feel nausea rising upward. I had been discharged with a prescription for muscle relaxants and pain medication, but I wouldn't be able to get them until the morning.

When I got home from the hospital, I saw a text from my neighbor offering help if needed. As soon as it was light, I would call her and ask her to pick up my prescription. But daylight was a long time away. Too long. It was hard to understand why the hospital staff, so eager to give me morphine, couldn't or wouldn't dispense the safest of pharmaceuticals to help me get through the night at home.

"There has got to be something in this house!" I said

to myself, trying to remember how many years it had been since I had taken over-the-counter pain killers.

"Ouch!"

A sharp muscle spasm in my torso thrust me back to the sofa. I could barely take a breath through the discomfort.

"Geez! God help me, please!"

God and my mind were the only resources I had to get me through the night.

I knew that tensing up and resisting pain would only make things worse. In theory, that all makes sense. But in practice, it's quite something else. Until you are in agony and attempting to surrender to pain for the first time, it is hard to imagine just how difficult it is. Most people hold their breath, which just makes things worse. I was no exception.

"Breathe. Relax. Let go," I told myself as I imagined my muscles and tissues softening.

Relaxing as best I could, I breathed into the area where the muscle spasms were most intense, imagining rich, oxygenated blood flowing into the bruised areas around my ribs and lower back. Then I exhaled as slowly as I could. I imagined what it would feel like as the cramps and tension let go and my muscles released into their normal, healthy state.

I imagined a pain meter, a big dial marked in increments of five from 0 to 100. Visualizing discomfort near 100 on the dial, I counted backward in fives, turning the dial down. I imagined how I would feel as the pain lessened.

After a few moments, the intensity of the discomfort

eased, and I began working on relaxing my throbbing scalp, puffy face and bruised eyelids. Then my aching arm and swollen fingers. Eventually the muscle spasms stopped and the pain diminished enough for me to get up off the sofa.

I hobbled to the guest bathroom in search of pharmaceutical relief, and opened the medicine cabinet that I had stocked when I moved into the house the year before. I had tried to think of everything a guest might need—toothpaste, toothbrushes, cotton balls, cosmetic puffs, needle and thread, Band-Aids, sunburn creams, triple antibiotic ointments, cold remedies, over-the-counter allergy and anti-diarrhea medications—but nothing for pain.

"What I would do for a shot of morphine, right now . . ." I lamented. At that moment, I regretted not staying in the hospital. But then I remembered the cats again.

Where are they?

I wanted to go outside and call for them. But first, I had to find something for the pain.   Eventually I remembered a small bottle of Advil in my travel bag in the master bathroom.

Draped in my yellow blanket, I shuffled back across the dimly lit family room toward the master suite in pursuit of pain relief. As I opened the double doors, bright light struck my bruised puffy eyes and took me completely by surprise. I stopped dead, gripped by fear, my heart pounding in my ears.

Someone is here! What else could it be?

I typically only use the soft bedside lamps in that

room. The only time I turn on the ceiling light with its four bright-white bulbs is to clean. Now it was the middle of the night and ALL the lights were on.

"Who is there?" I yelled out. My heart was pounding wildly. I felt completely defenseless and I could feel panic rising.

"Calm down!" I told myself, grasping for control. "Breathe."

A few slow deep breaths later, I remembered that during his walkthrough, the policeman had turned on all the lights. When he left, I shut the bedroom doors to keep the draft from coming through the broken window.

I stood at the doorway, taking in the scene. Small specks of broken glass littered the wood floor, glistening in the light. Glass fragments glinted on the white bed cover and the small matching rug next to the bed. A sudden gust of frigid wind blew through the shattered window. My heart clenched, and I froze.

Rationally, I could make the case that no one was there and that I was safe. Nevertheless, I was too afraid to take a step beyond the threshold of the door. I was paralyzed.

Eventually, I collected myself and took a deep breath. Then I turned around and retreated to the comfort, safety and neutrality of the family room sofa.

"I'll be okay. I don't need to go in there now," I told myself.

Unconsciously, I put out my right arm to help ease my aching body into the sofa.

"Aaaah!" I shrieked as unbearable pain shot up my arm, reminding me of the bruised, fractured bones.

I looked toward the master suite and realized I had left the doors open. If I didn't close them, the entire house would get cold. And getting that Advil couldn't hurt either. But I was simply too afraid to go back there.

What are you afraid of, Mandy? There is no one there, nothing that can hurt you now. You are safe!

I remembered the dream I had earlier about the Tokolosh. In South Africa's Zulu and Xhosa traditions, the Tokolosh is a scary, zombie-like, evil spirit.   Used in witchcraft, it is blamed for many things that go wrong in people's lives, evoking terror amongst those who believe in its existence.

I reminded myself that my attacker was in jail and that the likelihood of my getting attacked again, in this house, that night, was almost zero. I told myself that my imagination was making a bad situation worse.

Remember the Tokolosh and how the bed-on-bricks mythology came to be!

I   forced   myself   to   acknowledge   that the Tokolosh didn't really exist. It was created to explain mysterious deaths of people living in traditional mud huts. All too often, people sleeping close to the floor would die, whereas those who slept at a higher level survived, "escaping the Tokolosh."

The scientific explanation is that in cold weather, tribespeople burned cattle dung in their huts for warmth.

Burning cattle dung releases powerful toxic gases, including carbon monoxide. With the hut entrance closed to keep out the wind, these huts had no ventilation – nowhere for the carbon monoxide to go. Because the deadly gas is heavier than air, it accumulates closer to the ground. Naturally, the closer to the ground a person slept, the more quickly they were poisoned by the gas.

A lack of understanding of these mysterious deaths caused tribespeople to believe that the sudden demise of otherwise healthy people, many of them children, was caused by a (short) evil spirit. And so, the Tokolosh was born. People raised their beds, hoping that they would be out of its reach. Whenever unexplained difficulties arose, people blamed the Tokolosh. The more fearful they were, the more "bad" things happened and the more fearful they became. Proof of the wicked creature's existence was simply a matter of belief influencing action, influencing outcome, much like the placebo effect.

I knew that if I was going to get through this, I had to gain control of my mind. Blowing things out of proportion and making them scarier than they were was natural for this situation. But I could not afford to allow fear to consume me. I had to push back.

I reminded myself that if the mind can make things worse, it can also make those same things better. That is what I wanted to do. I decided that I had to go back to the master suite and prove to myself that there was no one there—that I was safe. There seemed to be no reasonable alternative.

Now, if I can just muster up the internal resources to get myself back there.

Mining for Resources

The quickest way I have found to access internal resources is to remember a time when those resources were plentiful and accessible to you. Then imagine stepping into *that you.*

> *Right now, what I need most is . . . courage. I need to be brave.*

I had found ways to be resourceful and brave for as long as I could remember. I tried to plug into those memories, like when I was sixteen and ready to take on the world. I remembered how my sister Cheryl and I sat cross-legged on the living room floor, foreheads touching, as Leo Sayer's "When I Need You" wafted out from the stereo speakers. I looked into Cheryl's brown eyes, her pretty face, framed by dark hair in a Cleopatra-cut.

Cheryl could only visit on Saturdays, the day my mother and stepfather went to the horse races, because she had been banned from the house for breaking the rules. She brought her beloved vinyl records with the latest hits from the US and the UK, along with a dose of sisterly advice and courage. She urged me to act on my dream of leaving South Africa and going to college in the United States. My father, who owned a travel agency, said he would get me a ticket and help make it happen.

"You should go. Things are too crazy to stay here," she said.

She is right. I should go.

I was only sixteen and the thought of travelling alone to the other side of the world, where I knew no one, was pretty scary. But I didn't want to let her see that. I would be brave. I would go.

A few days after my seventeenth birthday, dressed in a three-piece, ivory-colored, linen skirt-suit that matched the Samsonite luggage I borrowed from my grandmother, I boarded a South African Airways jumbo jet that was headed for the United States.

It took watching several episodes of *Dallas* to decide on just the right outfit for my trip. I knew that New York City was not Dallas, but how different could it be? Under the tailored waistcoat, I wore a chocolate brown shirt to go with my knee-high cowboy boots.

It never occurred to me that it might be dangerous, difficult or unwise to travel halfway around the world on my own, and no one thought to tell me. As strict as my mother could be about some things, when it came to big decisions like what to do with my life (or how to dress for a nineteen-hour flight to New York City) I was treated like the adult I thought I was.

I didn't really know where I was going or what to expect when I got there. But whatever it was, I was up for it. It would all turn out fine.

Stepping into that me, I immediately felt better and more confident.

I can do this! Yes, I am afraid, but that doesn't need to stop me. It will all turn out okay.

Putting my mind to work, I visualized the bedroom as I had seen it a few moments before. In my mind, I scanned the wood floor, the rugs, the low, modern leather bedframe, and the white bedcover accented by red and charcoal throw pillows. This time however, I imagined the lighting softer and more welcoming. I pictured myself walking safely through the bedroom into the bathroom. I noticed the spaciousness of the high ceilings, the scent of lavender coming from the candle next to the big tub, and the soothing pastel colors.

Relaxing into the experience, I visualized myself calmly passing the broken window, and noticing how well the policeman had secured it so that no one could get in. I imagined looking in every corner, seeing only what was familiar to me and no signs of danger.

I envisioned how it felt to be safe and confident, standing in the bathroom. Then I visualized myself opening the cabinet where my travel case was, and finding the Advil. Feeling how happy I would be when I accomplished the mission, proud of my courage and resilience. Then I lingered for a while in that feeling.

After replaying that scenario a few times in my mind, I was able to go back in. This time, I walked slowly but surely through the double doors, dimmed the bedroom lights, and made my way into the bathroom.

Suddenly I noticed glass and a pool of dried blood in one of the sinks. I gasped out loud and realized that my attacker must have cut himself when he came through the window and used the sink to clean up.

I was surprised again when I caught sight of myself in the mirror. The swelling from the bruises, bumps and cuts on my face made me almost unrecognizable.

"Don't go there. Stay focused!" I told myself, pushing the intrusive thoughts and judgments to the side. "We are on a mission."

Just as I had visualized, I opened the cabinet where my travel case was, and found the Advil where I pictured it to be. Mission accomplished! Not quite . . .

Yes, I had pushed through my fear and found my prize. But it had a child-proof cap on it, one that required you to pinch the sides of the cap and push it down at the same time. With my right hand and arm in a cast all the way to my shoulder, and bruised, swollen fingers, I didn't have the functionality or strength to get the cap off. I fumbled around, trying all types of maneuvers and contortions to open the bottle.

All at once, I saw the humor of the last twenty minutes.

You idiot! You forgot to visualize TAKING the damn pill. You'd think after twenty-plus years, you would know how to do this stuff!

I had been using visualization techniques since the mid-nineties, after I learned first-hand, through a series of epiphanies, how thoughts impact our experience. Those understandings caused me to change my life. Without analysis or trepidation, at a time when the personal coaching industry was in its infancy, I followed my intuition and became a business consultant and success coach, enthusiastically promoting human potential.

I wanted to do something radically different and became obsessed with the idea of making a positive difference in the world by helping people change their thinking habits. Because a lot of our thinking revolves around the pictures we create in our minds, and how we talk to ourselves, visualization and auto-suggestion are both important aspects of making those changes.

A fricking genius you are not!

Laughing at myself as much as my bruised ribs would allow, I made my way back to the patio door with the still unopened bottle of Advil in my hand. I opened the sliding door and called for the cats again, imagining them coming home safely. Then I went back to my makeshift sofa bed and, having had a good dose of laughter medicine, I put myself to sleep.

The cat door burst open, alarming me out of a fitful doze. It was 5:20 AM. Sophia sauntered in, like a runway model showing off a designer coat. Her big, green eyes were wide and captivating, and her long tail stood up in the air, swishing from side to side. Mako followed, loudly expressing his discontent.

All traces of pain and discomfort vanished for a few moments. My babies were home. They were cold, hungry and not at all pleased about spending the night out in the cold. But they were safe once again and despite everything else, my heart sang with joy.

Why?

"**D**o you think I did something to cause this, Sensei?" I asked Sensei Al, my Zen teacher who stopped by with flowers the day after the attack.

"Of course not," he said.

"Well then, why would something like this happen to me? It just seems so random!"

"It's natural to want life to make sense and have some type of logical explanation for everything. But there are some things that can't be explained. It is not your fault," he said with compassion.

Despite his assurances, I couldn't help wondering if I bore some responsibility for what had happened. I wasn't the only one. After the incident, many associates who were Law of Attraction enthusiasts asked me if the attack could have been a manifestation of a deeply held fear.

Apparently fear of attack inside one's own home is quite common, particularly among single women. But the thought of such an event happening to me had NEVER crossed my mind.

I had witnessed hundreds of real-life examples of the creative power of thought. No matter how much I tried to get it out of my mind, or people I respected tried to reassure me it wasn't so, the nagging question remained: Was this bizarre incident totally random or had I done something to provoke it?

Now I felt like a failure, afraid that, at some level, I had done something wrong, that I was at least partially to blame for the disaster my life had become. I thought about how I came to be living in Melbourne, how difficult the prior year had been and my recent experience with what people might call the Law of Attraction.

Five years previously, after relationships with one too many Peter Pan types, I decided to "Manifest my Soulmate." I concluded that unlike some of my previous picks, my ideal man would be mature, stable, dependable and secure. After making a list of required qualities, I redid my Match.com profile and put myself "out there," using my visualization skills to attract Mr. Right into my life.

After a lot of dating, I met a man who checked off all the boxes and pursued me with the prescribed dose of persistence. Unlike many of the other partners I had chosen before, this was a man my parents could have picked for me. He was mature, conservative, reliable and safe.

Our relationship developed quickly. Within a year, we became "life partners" and moved in together into a beautiful 1940's home with a white picket fence, one block off Las Olas Boulevard, in one of Fort Lauderdale's most desired neighborhoods. With a man to love and appreciate me, I felt whole, believing that the relationship was the answer to everything that ailed me.

I reoriented my business to reduce my travel schedule, appear more mainstream and fit in with our new, more settled lifestyle. We were a great compliment to each other. Two halves made whole. Or so I thought.

A few months after we moved in together, I mailed out an eight-page, printed newsletter announcing my new life with my new "life partner" to three thousand of my most faithful followers. Not long thereafter, my partner announced a different plan.

"What do you mean, you've changed your mind?" I asked, more surprised than angry.

"I don't want this," Mr. Right said, sitting at his desk, gesturing at the surroundings, the sparkling pool and the remodeling plans spread out in front of him. "It's too much . . . I'm overwhelmed."

We were in the master suite that looked out over the tropical oasis that was our backyard, in the home we had lived in for less than a year. He had been under a lot of stress due to the unexpected illness and death of a close family member. I could see him cracking under the weight of all the decisions he needed to make and the responsibility that had been thrust upon him.

I wanted to support him but selling the house now made absolutely no sense. We had been very happy there, and I knew he was overwhelmed and overreacting.

I looked straight at him and said, "Honey, this is not the time to be making life-changing decisions. You are under way too much stress. Let's take the remodeling off the table. We don't have to do that now—it can wait forever, as far as I am concerned. Let's take this one day at a time."

But his walls were up. "No. I've decided to put the house on the market. It will take a while for it to sell and you can stay here until it does."

What?

Until then it wasn't clear to me that I was included in the "this" that he no longer wanted and was "too much," a disposable item to be discarded. I was devastated, angry, confused. A million thoughts screamed in my head, but I was too upset to share them.

I thought about the newsletter I had just sent out and all the changes I had made in my business for the sake of our relationship.

How can this be happening to me?

I put my head in my hands, choking on tears.

"This is so humiliating!"

"Humiliating?" He sounded really surprised. "What do you mean? How is this humiliating? People break up all the time."

I stormed out of the room in tears.

Night sweats woke me at 2AM the next morning. Going through menopause, they had become a familiar occurrence. But this time was different: instead of putting myself back to sleep, as was my usual practice, I allowed my angst to take over. Indulging in fearful worst-case scenarios, I opened the door and let the Tokolosh in. He came carrying lots of baggage, all the pain of the past, and taunted me with the uncertainty of the future.

At first, the Tokolosh was manageable, like a good houseguest, emerging only in the quiet hours of the early morning.   Regurgitating fear, he fed on my heartbreak, doubts and insecurities.

When day broke, I pushed him away and he scuttled off into the shadows, but only for a while. Each time he returned, he stayed a little longer. The more I pushed, the bolder and more pervasive he became. Eventually, he took over completely and I became his slave.

Shocked, upset and humiliated, I was burning up in a raging fire fueled by menopausal emotion. I didn't feel like I could cope with nightly news let alone all THIS. I would need to find somewhere to live again. Where would I go? What would everyone think? How would I explain it?

The confidence, resilience and resourcefulness I had access to in earlier years were now bound and chained. I was a mess. Gaping wounds of unworthiness began to fester and I retreated into shame, alone.

At first, I told no one what was happening. But it seemed as if wherever I went, I would see someone I knew and they would ask about my "new" life with my "life-partner."

What life? What partner?

I didn't want to be seen, questioned and put under a microscope. I wanted to hide. Struggling with bouts of deep depression, I became preoccupied with my failures.

How could I help others, when my life was a disaster, a failure?

I felt like an imposter, who'd lost whatever credibility I had to do my work. I stopped calling myself a success coach.

Overwhelmed and consumed by shame, I fled with my two cats, landing in central Florida where no one knew me. Working from home, I managed to shut myself off from the world so much that days could pass without needing to see a soul. Just the way I wanted it. A self-imposed exile.

I bought a house and hunkered down, keeping only my favorite clients, most of whom had been with me for five or more years, and re-focused on the internet-related pieces of my business that allowed me to remain unseen. I was miserable.

But as Confucius said, "No matter where you go, there you are." And there I stayed. Alone, a prisoner of my past, beating myself up for all the mistakes and wrong decisions I had made.

Resistant to everything that was going on in my life, my self-loathing was relentless. So much so, that living with myself became quite unbearable.

I knew I had to do something. Before this breakup had drowned my self-concept, I'd meditated daily for twenty years and it had been enormously helpful in every aspect of my life. But for the last year or so, I was in such a dark place that I struggled to quiet my mind for even short periods.

I decided to join the Zen Center in the hopes that a

regular sitting practice, surrounded by other people, could bring me some peace. One of the benefits of Zen meditation is that you learn to come to terms with whatever is going on in your life and accept what is.

Gradually, with regular meditation, my inner state began to improve somewhat and I was coming to terms with my business situation and the failed relationships. I still had a way to go to get back to my happy pre-breakup self, but I was making good progress. That is, until this madman crashed into my life and turned everything upside down again.

Had my self-loathing somehow manifested a brutal beating from a total stranger while the police sat outside in their squad cars?

Aftershock

Sipping cold coffee through a straw, I lay on my sofa in a daze, my casted arm propped on a pillow. Sophia curled up on my lap, her silky black coat covering the blood-stained yellow blanket, her nose nestled between my thighs. Still on guard, Mako perched on top of the sofa cushion, purring loudly behind my head, his white socks and long whiskers on display. After a night out in the cold, he wasn't letting me out of his sight.

It was hard to move. Besides, I didn't want to. The physical pain was one thing. The mental loss from the concussion was another. I would hobble into a room to get something and then, finally arriving at my destination, have no idea where I was, or why I was there. For months after the attack, I couldn't add single digits, follow a movie plot or watch a TV show without getting lost.

I was worried about my business and whether it could survive this. I had recently taken on a new tech partner and agreed to give her a substantial monthly draw. Even though Lourdes had urged me to postpone a decision on our launch, I knew there was no choice but to cancel.

How would the bills get paid? How would we manage?

Three days after the incident, the police left a voice message saying that Ken Johnson, the attacker, had been released on bond. At the hospital, the policeman had assured me that they would never let him out on bail. With multiple serious charges against him, including a first-degree felony, the policeman had promised, "He is never getting out."

The attacker lived half a mile from my home. Obviously, he knew where I lived.

How dare they let him out! What if he comes back? Why did he come here in the first place?

Before getting that call, the Trauma Therapy techniques I had used when I got home from the hospital had worked marvelously. As difficult as my situation was, with the application of visualization exercises, fear was under control. But that changed as soon as I heard the message. The news that my attacker was out of jail triggered panic, and I couldn't get the brutality I'd experienced out of my mind. Believing my life could actually be in danger again, I couldn't reapply the solutions I had used previously.

"What if he comes back to finish the job?" my mother asked.

She had driven up from Miami after her pickleball game to help me get by. Dressed in sporting gear, her long, blond hair pulled back and her petite frame consistently poised for action, it was hard to believe she was eighty.

Not wanting her to freak out, I had underplayed what had happened.

"There was a break-in at my house and my right arm

is broken. Do you think you can come up for a few days to help me out?"

At the first sight of me, bruised and beaten, Mom, who is typically emotional and expressive, was unusually stoic. I can only imagine what must have been running through her mind. I was her caretaker. It was now up to her to take care of me: a reversal of the reversed roles we played.

I had brought my mom from South Africa to live with me in 1998. At that time, my sister Gail was battling a rare lung disease. Before she died, Gail shared her concerns about our mother. We agreed that it would be in everyone's best interest for Mom to come to the US and live with me.

Since I had left South Africa when I was seventeen to come to the US on my own, I knew it would be a big adjustment for both of us. And it was. We were both fiercely independent. We did our best to make things work, but after about a year of our strong, clashing personalities side-by-side, our living situation became intolerable.

Mom moved into an apartment and I encouraged her to develop interests of her own. Though already in her mid-sixties at that time, she found competitive venues and took up race-walking, running, table tennis and pickleball.

All her life she had dreamed of becoming a competitive athlete, but her parents had not allowed it. Instead, she married at seventeen, and by the time she was twenty-five, she had five children to raise. Now she had another opportunity to have the life she wanted.

When she was taking care of me after the attack, our

old relationship issues returned.

"Why don't you like me?" Mom would often ask.

I couldn't answer because I didn't know. It had been that way between us for as long as I could remember. Our time together was always strained and contentious. The instant she entered the room, my defenses went up. And vice versa.

Her financial dependency on me over the years seemed to make our relationship worse. She felt like I was in control of her life and I carried her responsibility like a cross.

The friction between us made it difficult for friends to be around the two of us together. As much as we both tried, it was hard to have a conversation that didn't end in an argument. It wasn't for lack of trying or lack of love. Hundreds of times, I'd consciously tried to shift the tension between us and create a loving environment. It never lasted long.

"I can't believe they let him out," she said. "How do you know he won't come back to kill you. Doesn't he live around the corner?"

"He won't, Mom. Don't worry, there is a restraining order and he is not allowed back here." Silently, I wondered what good a restraining order would do in a situation like this, but I didn't want to make my mom more afraid than she already was.

"Please, let's try to be positive," I said, looking in the pantry for a bottle of vodka.

"What do you want me to make for dinner?" she asked.

"Make whatever you want for yourself. I'm not hungry."

"You just don't like my cooking. Why won't you let me do anything for you?"

"Better make it a double," I whispered under my breath, reaching for the Absolut.

Though I tried to be brave around my mother, the knowledge that my attacker was free to roam the street shook me to the core. Even with muscle relaxants and pain killers, I was in too much physical discomfort to get a good night's rest. Sleep deprivation made all my other symptoms worse.

Occasionally I surrendered to deep bouts of unconscious exhaustion, but goaded by the Tokolosh, relief never lasted very long. Almost immediately, I would drift into a nightmare and sit up in terror, my heart racing, alert and alone in the dark, watching the shadows creeping across the ceiling.

Shame and Blame

Elizabeth sat at the end of the sofa rubbing my feet gently with arnica ointment, compassion pouring out of her bright blue eyes. Her soft, beautiful face was framed by long blond hair. It was four days since the attack, and her kind, loving presence comforted me like a warm bath on an icy day.

We had met at the Zen Center and I was immediately attracted to her light and warmth.

"Why didn't you call me?" she asked, horrified that I had come home from the hospital alone to an empty house after the attack.

"I didn't have your number. I didn't have my cell," I explained, withholding the truth that it hadn't occurred to me that I could call.

"We are in the phone book," she said.

Elizabeth is a psychotherapist, retreat leader and interfaith minister. Over the past year, I had gone to her for some private sessions and attended several of her talks and group programs. As a result, she knew some of my history and had glimpsed my old wounds that begged for healing— wounds that I was not ready to expose.

"Maybe this will be an opportunity for you to do some deep healing," she said sweetly. Her softly spoken words felt like lashes whipping my bruised psyche. My defenses came up immediately. I could feel the muscles around my chest tighten, and a cold veil of resistance washed over my eyes. This was the last thing I wanted to hear.

I took a deep breath and said nothing.

It seemed that the words and actions of the people I interacted with during the first few weeks of recovery only made things worse. I could not come to terms with the fact that something like this had happened to me.

Since moving to Melbourne, blessed with great health, I had not taken the time to establish myself with a primary doctor. Now my insurance company required me to get referrals from a primary care physician to get the treatment I needed.

Unable to get an immediate appointment as a new patient with a medical doctor, I eventually found a physician assistant at a busy medical center, who could see me about a week after the incident.

With an open wound gaping in the bottom lip of my heavily bruised, swollen face, I shuffled painfully along the corridor, carrying my broken arm in the overpriced blue sling purchased in the emergency room. I was disheveled, dressed in old sweat pants, a flimsy muscle shirt and a warm shawl—the only clothes I could physically manage to get into. Most people averted their eyes and pretended not to see me.

What are they thinking?

Passersby who made eye contact would often offer a variation of "hate to see what the other guy looks like." I had lost my sense of humor. The euphoric sense of gratitude I'd experienced immediately after my escape from the house had drowned in a sea of pain and anxiety.

My new physician was a young, pretty brunette who didn't look old enough to have graduated from college. In addition to the other injuries the hospital staff had noted in my medical record, she was concerned that my nose was broken, so she referred me to an Ear Nose and Throat specialist in the same facility.

Filling out the umpteenth medical form of the day with my left hand, I responded to the "reason for your visit" question with my own question in a staccato scribble: "Is my nose broken?"

After a long wait, the young ENT walked into the room. Tall, slender and self-assured, he appeared to be in his mid-thirties. He looked at my beaten face and glanced at the demographics on my chart.

"So, you are here to see if your nose is broken?" He let out a deep sigh as though answering a five-year-old who had asked the same question for the twelfth time.

"I wouldn't worry about it," he said. "It takes a much younger man to break a facial bone."

Did I hear that right? Why does he think it was an old guy who beat me up? Surely, he is not insinuating . . . ?

I was stunned by his implication and even more surprised by my own reaction.

Shame washed over me. Yes, shame! Then anger.

"The guy who hit me is twenty-one," I said defensively.

"How do you know him?"

"Know him? What do you mean? I was assaulted during a home invasion."

"Well, let's take a look then."

My nose wasn't broken, but I felt like I was. Between the attack, lack of sleep, and anxiety over money, health, and safety, my psyche was incredibly fragile.

I imagined that all those people who were averting their eyes when they saw me were probably thinking the same thing. I was embarrassed to think that people had judged me to be a battered woman, a victim of domestic abuse. Then I felt guilty about THOSE feelings.

"How could I be so judgmental about victims of abuse?" I moaned to Lourdes, who acted as my anchor in the weeks following the attack, keeping me afloat from two hundred miles away. "What made my situation better?"

If you were ever drowning, Lourdes is the person you'd want on the rescue ship. Not because she knows about boats—I'm not even sure if she swims. But when it comes to navigating the turbulent waters of life, she is the strongest captain you could want. You might try to beat her off with a paddle (and believe me, I tried), but she continues, undeterred, holding your head above the water.

Lourdes found me a personal assistant on Craigslist, pushed me to get Trauma Therapy, and coaxed me out the house to "get fresh air." Mostly, she listened.

There were times when I loved her and couldn't wait for our talks. And there were times when she made me so angry that I never wanted to speak to her again. One of those times occurred a few weeks after the "incident."

"Who knows what was in those drugs?" she had said after reading the police report stating that the assailant was under the influence of LSD. "What a horrible situation this must be for him and his family."

She had researched Ken's background on the internet and discovered that he was from a "normal" family, an Eagle Scout, a senior at Florida Institute of Technology.

I did not realize at the time that she was researching his history to make sure that with him out on bond I was not in any immediate physical danger. She wanted to help me feel safe so I could sleep at night without worrying that he was coming back to kill me.

When my physical safety no longer seemed to be an issue to her, she pushed me to begin the hard work of emotional healing.

"One wrong decision and his life is ruined," she said, speaking of my attacker, with what I interpreted to be the same empathy and compassion she had shown to me. "You are going to need to work on releasing this, on forgiving him—"

"What! Forgive him? Did you not see the pictures of my face? Do you realize what he did? He almost killed me!" I was furious.

"Yes, I know, but your anger is poisoning you. You're going to have to release it if you want to heal."

That was not what I wanted to hear. Tears welled up and my throat closed.

"I have to go," I said, and hung up the phone. For several days, I let her calls go to voicemail.

When I got the police report, I was shocked to discover that the police had been sitting outside my house throughout the attack. Two officers had responded to a domestic dispute call from another neighborhood. My attacker fled on foot and broke into my home to escape the police.

The police witnessed him breaking my fence and window, and saw him enter my home. While I was getting the crap beaten out of me, the Melbourne police were parked outside, waiting for backup. I was appalled!

After weeks of waiting for an appointment, I went to see a neurologist for prolonged symptoms of concussion, including loss of memory and analytical skills. My arm was still in a cast and it was difficult to dress and drive. There was no parking when I got to the medical center, and when I finally got to the physicians' office, exhausted from the effort, I was almost ten minutes late.

"I am sorry," his assistant said, "you're late. Our policy is not to take patients who come in late. You will have to set up another appointment."

"What?" I said as tears of frustration ran down my face. There were no other patients in the waiting or examining room and I could see the doctor sitting behind his desk, in his office. I refused to leave and eventually he agreed to examine me.

It was soon after the Republican primaries and Donald Trump was at the head of the pack in central Florida. When the neurologist, a bespectacled, middle-aged white man, heard my story he immediately asked, "Did they catch the guy?"

"Yes," I said. "But he is out on bail."

"I bet the guy who did this was one of those immigrants. Those illegals, they are the only ones who get away with this sort of thing."

Once again, I was bewildered. In my heaviest South African accent, I said, "No. He is as American as you are."

It turned out that the neurologist had been involved with the athletic department at Florida Institute of Technology, so when I mentioned that the attacker was on the track team there, naturally he wanted to know more.

Suddenly, I felt strangely protective of my attacker. I wanted him to be judged for what he had done, not for his ethnicity or race. As a white person growing up in South Africa during apartheid, I understood the dangers of prejudice. Even though I had left the country when I was young, there is a part of me that bears the collective shame of the society I was inadvertently a part of. I was careful not to use the assailant's name nor mention that he was black.

I didn't know if the physician was racist or not, but given what I judged as his bigoted remark about immigrants, I didn't want to find out. From my perspective, the thought of my pain being used to confirm someone's racial bias was almost as bad as the attack itself.

"You have a heart murmur, you know," he said, with his stethoscope poised on my chest. "I hope now you will get your security situation taken care of."

What is it that makes people so quick to judge that this situation was somehow my fault? Is it because we inherently believe that nothing happens to us that we don't will or deserve? Or, is it a defense people use to convince themselves that this type of thing couldn't happen to them personally or to someone they love?

Leaving the office, he cautioned me: "Remember, don't block with your head."

I fantasized rushing him, head first, and taking him out.

Instead, I bought the URL "StupidOutLoud.com" thinking I would use this experience as an opportunity to educate people on the dos and don'ts of what to say when people are sick, injured or have lost a loved one.

Most people don't mean to add insult to injury, but when we are emotionally fragile, even well-intended, thoughtful comments can feel like a crushing blow.

I realized it was hard for people to accept that this violent act had taken place quite randomly.

How could a break-in happen in the middle of the day, on a Sunday? What kind of criminal would choose to break into a locked, occupied house in the middle of a block, in a quiet, safe neighborhood when people are likely to be at home and awake? Especially in Florida, a state where many people own guns and understand our Stand Your Ground laws?

It didn't make sense! And people can't protect themselves from things they don't understand. They wanted to feel safe. And they wanted me to give them assurance that something like this couldn't or wouldn't happen to them.

"That is why I have a dog," the medical assistant said while drawing my blood.

"I am glad I know self-defense!" said a friend at the gym.

They wanted an explanation. They wanted to believe that they would be safe.

"What do you think you could have done to stop it?" asked a fellow Zen practitioner.

"Why did he choose your house?" a business associate wanted to know, as if I was hiding a secret motive that could explain the randomness of the whole bizarre incident.

The more questions people asked, the more I felt judged and the more I judged myself. I wondered if at some unconscious level I bore some responsibility for what had happened.

Part 2: Spring of Hope

Taming the Tokolosh

Heart pounding and terrified, I woke up in the middle of the night. Every noise triggered a horror movie in my mind. Staring at the ceiling, I'd count backward from 100 to 1, telling myself, "I am calm, relaxed and in control." Then I'd get up and check the doors again.

After the call that alerted me to my attacker's release, I stopped trying to manage anxiety. Fear took on a life of its own and became more generalized. I needed only to turn on the television to find something cringe-worthy. I became preoccupied with the viciousness of the presidential elections, terrorist attacks, police killings and what I saw as the unleashed rage of average Americans. Physical safety was now the least of my concerns.

The more I fed my fear, the more it grew, the more "attacked" I felt, the more separated and terrified. The Tokolosh was running my life and I felt powerless to do anything about it.

At the insistence of Lourdes, I finally got Trauma Therapy by two very capable therapists, Louise Peters and Rachel Lefebvre. Luckily, I knew them personally so they agreed to treat me at home given that I was unable to leave the house. Both used techniques that bypass the conscious mind—in my opinion, an important aspect of effective Trauma Therapy.

Within a few weeks, the uncontrollable panic and irrational anxiety, both symptomatic of PTSD, dissipated. But I knew that there was a lot more work to do.

Obviously, you can't solve a problem unless you identify it. And that is one of the advantages of a regular meditation practice. It forced me to look at things I might otherwise avoid through constant "busyness" and distraction.

After the assault, even though I couldn't truly meditate, I continued the practice of sitting still every morning for a half-hour or so. Sometimes I listened to guided meditations, sometimes I imagined myself sitting in a sacred garden, and at other times, I just sat quietly as my mind spun around like a figure-skating ballerina doing the freestyle.

The daily routine of observing my thoughts made me realize how much we human beings add to our own suffering. I saw how my own craziness made things worse for me. I knew I had to accept what was happening and let go of my resentment toward the attacker and the police. But I felt incapable of doing anything about it.

Things finally began to shift when Elizabeth offered to perform a spiritual cleaning of my house. It never occurred to me that the ritual would materially change anything. Still homebound, I thought it might provide a welcome interruption to the inertia of my life. I gladly accepted.

In the days leading up to the spiritual cleansing ceremony, I meditated on Lourdes's comments about forgiving the attacker.

In the past, I had done a lot of forgiveness work and had first-hand experience of its healing powers. So much so, that years prior, I had created a guided visualization audio on forgiveness that was sold at my seminars and on my website.

You don't need to be highly evolved to WANT to forgive. You just need to recognize how horrible anger, hatred and resentment make you feel inside. Resentment is a cancer that negatively impacts your whole life, hurting and punishing you continually, every you time you think about the incident—long after it is over. How does that serve you?

I knew Lourdes was right. Forgiving my attacker was key to my own emotional healing, but I was not ready. People struggling with how to forgive someone often get stuck because they think that by forgiving, they are condoning what that person did. But that is simply not the case. The goal of forgiveness is to liberate and bring peace to the person who feels the anger.

Knowing that I needed to let go of the negative emotions did nothing to lower my resistance to the idea. I had the necessary tools at my disposal but not the motivation to use them. To solve this problem, I decided that instead of working on forgiveness per se, I would simply work on softening my positions, and increasing my DESIRE to let go of the resentment I felt.

Resentment eats you up inside. It does nothing to harm the person who hurt you. All you need to do to realize this, is to spend ten minutes sitting alone, focused on the feelings of resentment you feel. It won't take long for you to WANT a change.

I began using a few minutes of my sitting meditation practice to simply observe how the anger and resentment made me feel. Then I'd compare that to joyful and expansive feelings of unconditional love or friendliness, like those I have for my adorable cat Sophia. I would then encourage my desire to forgive with a question such as,

How would it feel to be this open-hearted toward everyone I am in contact with?

Typically, negative emotions like anger, grief, frustration and overwhelm all have different qualities and are experienced physically in different ways. Everyone is different in how they experience these emotions. For me, anger is experienced as tightness and heat in my chest, and as a numbing sensation around my forehead and temples.

Developing awareness and working with negative feelings is not easy because it feels like you are willingly walking into a fire. But the truth is that walking over the hot coals is a lot easier than you might think. And certainly, a lot less painful than dealing indefinitely with the erupting volcanos your unresolved emotions will create for you throughout your life.

Because we find unpleasant feelings disagreeable,

people react by pushing them away and/or distracting themselves so they avoid them altogether. Not a healthy strategy in the long run. But if we can learn to give attention to those emotions, and work with them, we can, in fact, change them.

To encourage my willingness to let go of the animosity I was feeling, I worked on expanding sensations of unconditional friendliness by imagining my cat Sophia in front of me, and intensifying those good feelings. Then I would bring in friends, family members and clients, starting with those whom I felt the most warmth toward, sending them rays of understanding, friendliness and kindness.

How would it feel to have this level of compassion toward all beings?

Gradually I worked on adding people who had angered me into the mix. I would start with people who may have hurt me in a small, unintentional way, sending them a wish that they be happy and free from suffering.

Then I would do the same thing with people whom I found little harder to forgive, and as I did so, I would stop to acknowledge how much better I felt each time I was able to let go of negative emotions.

After a few days, my barriers became more pliable. As they did, I noticed myself becoming less self-righteous, more flexible, more open, more interested in being happy. I was still somewhat angry and resentful. The difference was that I *desired* that things would be different. As my desire grew, I began tapping into the huge arsenal of resources that I had accumulated over the years.

Whenever I got stuck in my judgment and anger, I would simply bring Sophia back into my awareness, focus on those good feelings, and try again, reinforcing to myself that this process was for me, to make me feel better, acknowledging that anger did not feel good inside me, and if given a choice, I choose to be happy.

Gradually I moved through my resistance and began to accept the situation I was in. As my resistance softened, and my internal dialogue improved, my fears began to calm down. I started choosing relaxing, uplifting music instead of the television news for background noise. I started to go outside, feel the sunshine, and look for signs of spring.

Signs of Spring

The "House Cleaning" ceremony took place about two months after the attack, on a beautiful Sunday afternoon. Incense wafted through the house as soft, dreamy music played in the background and fresh flowers graced every corner. Glowing in candlelight, my home felt warm and vibrant again.

Elizabeth led the ritual and followed Native American custom, smudging the house with sage and blessing every corner of my property. Friends from all over the country "held the space" with meditation and prayer. My friend Lynn, who was kind, attentive and supportive throughout my recovery, brought homemade cookies, and Lourdes drove up from Miami with her son. But most of the people who showed up and participated in the blessing of my home that day were strangers to me.

Quite unexpectedly, during one of the prayer rituals, I had a profound spiritual experience. Deep in meditation, I felt a heavy weight being lifted off me, and then it was gently replaced with a cloak of serenity. I saw a vision of my attacker surrounded in a golden light. In that instant, I felt that I had forgiven him.

This moment of Grace came without any effort on my part. I only contributed a strong desire for peaceful acceptance of what had happened, along with a willingness to let go.

Like a butterfly emerging from its chrysalis state, still hesitant and wobbly, I had the sense of coming alive once again. Though my arm was in a brace and my head still somewhat fuzzy, I began looking at life through a brighter lens.

Help poured in from all directions. Prayers, love and even money streamed in from friends, fans and total strangers across the country. The feelings of isolation that had plagued me since I moved to Melbourne two years earlier lifted like fog in sunlight.

When I returned to daily exercise, I was shocked at how much strength I had lost in the two and half months I had been sedentary. Having always identified with being a strong, healthy and physically fit person, the recent shift to a weak, broken and unfit body was intolerable, and I became determined to do something about it.

I started with walking the bridge across the Indian River. The first time I tried it, I could barely make it to the top. It was hard to get myself motivated, but with so many people rooting for me, I pushed through, telling myself that I couldn't let everyone down.

The next day I got up and tried again. It wasn't any better. But by the end of the week, I made it over and back. Not easily or quickly, but over. That small accomplishment strengthened my resolve and gave me confidence that I would bounce back.

In late April, my close friend Luanne came down from North Carolina to spend a few days. After the attack, I had a great deal of social anxiety, and up until her visit, avoided going to public places where there might be crowds of people. But somehow, she coaxed me out and we had fun. For the first time since the attack, I felt "normal." Quite naturally, my anxiety around groups of strangers diminished, and after she left, I ventured out alone, unafraid.

After a few more weeks, I went back to work, got a new haircut, returned to my Zen group and even went out on a date. Things were looking up.

Finally, I returned to yoga practice. Though I had been an enthusiastic yogi for many years, I now understood yoga at a very different level, using it to compliment the mindfulness practices I was engaged in. The physical practice became a working metaphor for the psychological work I was undertaking. At first, many of the postures that were easy before felt impossible. But I kept reminding myself to breathe into the resistance—instead of fighting it—just as I had done the night I got home from hospital to alleviate physical pain. As I relaxed and softened, I grew stronger, more open and more flexible.

I was ready to write a happily-ever-after ending for this chapter of my life. What I didn't realize was that the work was just beginning.

Part 3: Summer of Fire

Setback

If you are like me, you can probably identify with wanting the story to come to a happy ending. The sooner, the better. A desire for the smooth ascension of the story line, culminating in the happily-ever-after, a neat wrap-up that explains why things happened and proves that what we want to believe is true. But in real life that seldom happens, except perhaps in movies or books.

(But not this one.)

Sometimes, when life gets turned upside down, after the initial trauma, we get a glimpse of hopeful optimism. That light can carry you forward for quite a while. But eventually, you must start building your life over, brick by brick. It is then that the real work begins.

Recovery didn't come as quickly or as easily as I thought it "should." My broken arm led to problems with my wrist. I had a big painful lump in my head that wouldn't go away and a worrisome heart issue that I hadn't told anyone about.

Overnight I had gone from being vibrant and energetic to feeling old and beaten-down. I was in much better shape now than I had been immediately after the attack, but I couldn't escape the reality that I looked and felt like I had aged ten years.

I also lost my motivation for work, something that had never happened before. No matter how bad things had been in the past, I always loved work.

From a practical standpoint, the concussion made it hard for me to do my job effectively. My analytical skills were shot and my memory was mush. But more than the physical repercussions, what impaired me most was the loss of whatever sense of control I had had over my life. Everything seemed random, indiscriminate and unfair.

As I was dealing with all this, I checked in with the State Attorney about the pending criminal case. There never seemed to be any forward progress in the proceedings.

Incognito, I stalked Facebook to see what Ken Johnson was up to. Occasionally I checked the college website for his most recent athletic accomplishments.

It seemed to me that while I was struggling, his life had gone back to normal. He was touring with the track team, winning contests at school.

In May, he graduated.

By that time my support network, while still strong, had returned to their own lives and priorities. It was time for me to get back on my own two feet. I would get up most days with resolve and determination, but then slip quietly into frustration and overwhelm as the day progressed.

"Tomorrow will be better," I promised myself before I went to sleep. But tomorrow wasn't better, and as summer approached, I felt an increasing sense that my world was breaking apart.

In the wee hours of June 12th, after tossing and turning, unable to sleep, I got up, walked into the family room and turned on the television. There was breaking news happening about fifty miles from my home.

Omar Mateen, a twenty-nine-year-old man, had marched into the Pulse nightclub in Orlando with a semi-automatic weapon. Broadcast in real time, in high definition, I watched horrified, as victims, hiding in the bathroom and under tables, called 911 in terror, trying to escape Mateen's violent hatred. By the end of the night, forty-nine people, out for a good time on a Saturday night, were massacred. Fifty-eight others were wounded.

The murderous attack shook me to my core, triggering the terror and trauma I had experienced a few months previously. Fixated on the news coverage, I felt like I was experiencing the tragedy first-hand, feeling the suffering of the victims as if I were one of them.

The Tokolosh was back. He became a frequent, uninvited guest who showed up often, sometimes, when least expected, appearing from nowhere, like a conjurer, gripping my heart and putting me under the spell of fear.

Stopped at a red light, the stranger walking casually across the street suddenly turned into a threat. I locked my doors and looked away. I would be engrossed in a project, staring at my computer screen, and he would show up, without warning, to push me into a pool of financial anxiety.

Nighttime was always bad, but social gatherings once again became the worst. He taunted me from the other side of the room, showing me how broken and alone I was—and would always be. He compared me to all the others who seemed so "together," happy, connected, healthy and secure. I would turn my back and go home.

Convinced that I was being judged, criticized and attacked, I did what was my nature to do: I retreated. I put walls up and pushed the feelings away. But no matter how many times I told myself fear wasn't real, no matter how much I resisted, the Tokolosh returned, bolder, stronger and more menacing.

A few days after the Orlando killings, I got a Federal Express envelope from Ken Johnson's lawyer. Inside was a mitigation report he had filed with the court, requesting a downgrading of my attacker's sentence. He was asking that his client be put on probation and that adjudication be withheld for five years.

In the report, he laid out their case:

Up until that February day, Mr. Johnson had been an exemplary young man. He was an Eagle Scout, and had been a Class A volunteer firefighter since the age of seventeen. He had been popular in high school, named Prom King and Homecoming King, and was on scholarship to Florida Institute of Technology, where he was on the track team.

Mr. Johnson's aberrant behavior, his attorneys said, stemmed from his inability to handle peer pressure. His friends had egged him on to experiment with LSD, something he had never tried before. His reaction to the psychedelic drug was extreme and prolonged, and led to the "incident" at my house the following day.

They said that he had no recollection of what happened or what he had done to me.

How could he say he didn't remember?

I realized that up until then, my "forgiveness" had been conditional. It would allow for a reduced sentence—maybe even no prison time. But still there had to be consequences. He needed to "pay" for what he had done.

How dare he destroy my life and say he doesn't remember?

Everywhere I looked, I saw violence, viciousness, brutality, division and injustice. At the time, I didn't realize that the anxiety, heart palpitations and inability to focus were returning symptoms of PTSD, or I would have reached out to Louise, my Trauma Therapist, for help. Instead, I thought I "should" be "over it by now," and beat myself up for not being able to get back on the proverbial horse of my life. I became increasingly irritable, angry and unable to sleep, and except for daily phone and email contact with my business partner and occasional conversations with Lourdes, I withdrew from the outside world again.

Do I really want to live in this world?

I was not the only one thinking along those lines.

On June 27th, I got word that my sister Adrienne tried to commit suicide. We had spoken a couple weeks prior when I called my father in South Africa and she happened to be there visiting. We were never particularly close.

I was shocked by the news. Was there something I could have done or said to help her? Or worse, had I said something on that phone call that triggered her despair?

Soon after Adrienne got out of hospital, she set herself on fire and was lucky to survive.

I voiced my anxieties to my business partner, Toby. From my view point, we had become very close, and I considered her a confidante and friend. But I had misread the situation completely.

Without warning, Toby stopped returning my calls and emails. When I persisted, she sent me a "breakup email" in which accused me of playing "the victim," saying there was much too much drama in my life and she didn't want to be a part of it.

Her plan was to split the business and take the most profitable aspects that I had been paying her to work on for the past several months. When I refused her offer, she sabotaged the website and ultimately broke the web-based business we had been building.

Betrayed and wounded, I was stunned by what I interpreted as another vicious attack that seemed to come from nowhere.

I felt like I was in a pressure cooker, coming to an angry boil. I had had enough and I wasn't going to take "it" anymore. I would show them all: my attacker, the police, my ex-business partner, even my sister.

After drinking a bottle of wine, I sat down and wrote an email to a business attorney friend of mine to explore suing my now-ex business partner. Next, I wrote to the State Attorney's office expressing my outrage at the lawyer's request. Never ever ever would I agree to the mitigation request. Never, ever, EVER.

Then I put in a request to my attorney asking for a meeting with my attacker. I wanted to confront him. I wanted to give him a blow-by-blow account of what he had done to me and show him photos of all my injuries. I wanted an apology. More than anything, I wanted a do-over of that Super Bowl Sunday, one in which I never met Mr. Johnson and I continued to work peacefully at my desk.

Finally, my rage spent, I got into bed and pulled the covers over my head.

Missing Cowboy Suit

It was hard to get up. Nothing made sense anymore. Resistant and disempowered, it was as if I was awake in my own recurring nightmare, knowing I was dreaming but paralyzed and unable to get out of it. I was being pulled downriver in a fast-moving current, desperately grabbing at tree limbs, trying to resist the pull of the treacherous current and the inevitable danger of the whitewater rapids around the bend.

After all I'd been through with the attack, didn't I deserve a break?

It seemed like all my previous work had been for naught as I sank into darkness and depression. Looking at life through a veil of fear and disappointment, I saw my entire past as a succession of failures and bad decisions. Trapped in a cycle of guilt and self-admonishment, I conjured up images of a gloomy future I couldn't see a way through.

For two months, I buried myself in despair, wishing I could disappear, not wanting anything enough to act to get it.

With all the tools at my disposal, I have no one to blame but myself.

At this point in my recovery, everyone assumed I was getting back on my feet. I honestly thought that I could and "should" get my old life back. As if nothing had happened.

Come on, Mandy, put your cowboy suit on and let's do this.

But that part of me seemed to have disappeared, and what was left, couldn't make anything happen. I drank too much, ate too little and pulled back from the world again. My business was collapsing, my health was questionable and my faith was lost. I was too ashamed this time to reach out for help.

What is wrong with me?

To the extent I could, I kept up necessary appearances and held onto whatever business I still had left. After one of my monthly trips down to Miami, a very dear client sent me an email. She wrote,

"I hope you don't mind that I share a bit of my faith ... I see God's work in my life and the daily miracles He does for us and for many. Feeling loved by God has saved me and has made me want to know Him more.

I wish I could pass on the joys it brings to me. I am nothing without God!

I love you Mandy and I keep you and your family in my prayers."

My client is a busy physician who seldom sends me a personal email. Getting that type of email from her was a wakeup call. Not only did I realize how unsuccessful I was in keeping up appearances, I knew that I was in deep water. I had to do something or I would drown.

I didn't click the link she offered. Instead, I shut down my computer and sobbed like a baby, something I had not done in years.

Becoming the Diver

Many years ago, when I first consciously chose a spiritual path, I read a statement in an old book of Runes that I have pondered for years. It said, "When in deep water become the diver."

And dive I did. I stopped holding back, stopped resisting, stopped pretending. Instead I surrendered to the pent-up emotion that I had been trying to contain, pacify and ignore. And there was a lot to let go of.

After weeks of melancholy introspection, I finally owned up to the fact that what was happening "to" me was a projection of what was happening "in" me. This was not a new revelation given my history, training and experience. But when you are fumbling around in the dark, no matter how much knowledge or experience you have, it is difficult to see.

Maybe Toby had a point. Perhaps I am stuck in victimhood.

I realized that my troubles had started long before the attack. That the random beating I had gotten from Ken was nothing compared to how I beat up myself for mistakes made in the past. The anger and resentment I felt toward my business partner for leaving me in the lurch (and causing me substantial financial hardship) mirrored the guilt and punishment that I had inflicted on myself. My sister's suicidal acts played out my own feelings of self-destruction.

The deeper I dived, the more I realized that many of the *causes* I attributed to problems, were in fact, *effects*. The world becomes a mirror to show us our own unresolved feelings, and as I noticed that in myself, I began to see the same phenomena play out in the lives of my clients, friends and relatives.

I had not understood that emotional hygiene is at least as important as physical hygiene. I didn't realize that when you try to suffocate pain, it metastasizes and finds another way to manifest itself. And whatever we push down will keep coming back up, like heartburn, until we are ready to bring it out into the light and look at the cause.

In hindsight, I could see the exorbitant price my avoidance had cost me and how much trouble I could have saved myself by dealing with psychological discomfort when it arose. Now I had another chance, another choice to make.

"Who do I want to be?" I asked myself, realizing that I was at a crossroads—a decision point, another opportunity to turn things around.

I knew for sure that I did not want to be an angry, bitter person. I had seen too many old, unhappy people who lived in the past, nursing their grudges and grievances.

So, what does that look like? What do I want instead?

Then I caught myself.

Before I go to the "what next" I need to deal with "what is." Or I will be applying the same thinking that got me into this mess in the first place.

I dived back into the teachings, books and techniques that had worked for me in the past and made a critical decision: I would use what had happened as my wake-up call for deep healing, as Elizabeth had suggested right after the attack, and as Lourdes had been alluding to for years. I would stop focusing on what everyone else was doing and concentrate only on what was in my power to influence or control. Mainly, I decided to concentrate on my relationship with myself by healing whatever came up—instead of burying it in the basement. After all, I had nothing left to lose.

After I made the decision to take responsibility for my life and stop being a victim, I knew I had to tackle the Tokolosh somehow. I had to come to terms with the irrational fear and anxiety that had taken over my life.

Resistance, obviously, had not worked. It was time to try another approach. I had plenty of tools to work with. I just had to pick one. Regular therapy sessions would probably have been very helpful at that time, but I was feeling so much financial pressure that I couldn't or wouldn't justify the investment.

Recognizing how delicate I was, I decided to start with the gentle Tibetan practice of Tonglen.

Tonglen is the practice of letting go of negative feelings. Originating in India, it migrated to Tibet in the eleventh century. Literally, the Tibetan word means "sending and taking." More than a meditation practice, it is an attitude, a beautiful way of transmuting the pain of our lives into a sense of being connected to others.

When we see or feel suffering, we breathe in with the intention of completely feeling and accepting it. Then we send out a wish for an end to that suffering on the outbreath in the form of healing, compassion, loving-kindness— whatever encourages relaxation and openness. After working with your own pain, you turn your attention to others who are experiencing the same type of suffering. Though Tonglen is typically used in a sitting meditation practice, I prefer to use it when I am in motion.

Walking over the Indian River bridge, I breathed in the general anxiety I was feeling. Immediately, I felt myself tense and resist. Consciously I relaxed my body, trying to soften and open. A stray thought flew in to rescue me from feeling my fear. But this time, I didn't take the bait.

"Stay! Stay!" I reminded myself, opening up to feel the fear, as I inhaled once again. Then I exhaled very slowly, wishing myself love, compassion and safety.

Kindness toward myself had never come easily, and this process was like a cool fresh breeze in the summer heat. Having allowed myself to feel, it felt very comforting.

I continued this process, focused on my own feelings, for a few minutes, as I looked out at the big blue sky and made my way to the foot of the bridge. With every inhale, I felt a little more accepting, and with every exhale, a little less anxious, a little calmer.

Then I began to think of other people I knew, who

had also suffered this same type of feeling—friends, clients and family members. I even thought of my pets. I breathed in their suffering, their anxiety. Then on the exhale I sent them love, safety and peace.

As I walked to the top of the bridge, I expanded my subjects to include the forty million Americans who suffer from anxiety, wishing them relief.

By the time I made it to the far side of the bridge, I was sending out wishes of peace and tranquility to all the beings of the world who were fearful and afraid. I expanded that to dolphins, polar bears, monkeys, birds and critters of all kinds. I thought about people suffering in war-torn countries, on small, peaceful islands, in the jungles of the Amazon, the African bush and I even remembered the Eskimos, who worry about their future and their survival. The more love and peace I sent out to others, the calmer, more connected and whole I felt.

By the time I got back to my car, anxiety had alchemically transformed into compassion. Beneath the veil of separateness, I caught a glimpse of the breathtaking beauty of life, interconnected, interdependent and above all, shared.

The Heart of the Matter

It seemed that everywhere I turned, the subject of self-love came up. And when it did, I felt the familiar signs of resistance in my body.

What was that about? I began asking, working through the opposition instead of running away from it.

I'd always understood the value of self-confidence, but never self-love. To the old me, self-love seemed like a wimpy excuse for not living up to one's full potential and doing what needs to be done. The idea didn't seem to have any real, intrinsic value, other than to make you feel good in the moment.

How is that helpful, I thought, when there is so much to be accomplished, overcome and conquered? My strategy for success was hard-driving discipline, laden with guilt and self-admonishment.

From my current vantage point, life upside down, not knowing how I would survive and struggling just to get through the day, I realized that that approach hadn't worked out so well. It seemed insane to keep doing it.

"It's time to try something different," I told myself.

I thought about the struggles I had had with

relationships—with lovers, business partners, family members and others—and the concept of love. When we are in early stages of attraction, we focus on all the good things we love and admire about the other person. But when the relationship goes sour, it is typically because grievances—petty or otherwise—have obscured that loving vision.

Usually the things we object to are the very same qualities that attracted us to that person in the first place. So, what is it that causes those grievances? As I dived deep into the issue honestly, I realized that, in almost every case, fear was an underlying cause. And where fear lives, so does the Tokolosh.

There was fear of loss, money, looks, power, control, pride or safety. There was fear of rejection, fear of being alone, fear of failure, fear of success, fear of being judged, and fear of not being enough. And when fear comes up, we naturally erect a wall of protection that separates us from one another.

The love may still be there, on the other side of the wall, but we can no longer see it. Eventually, it moves out of our awareness completely.

If walls and avoidance create opposition to love, what needs to happen instead?

We cannot heal through walls of resistance or fear. We can only heal what we can be with and bring into the light. In the darkness, we go numb, and create fertile ground for the Tokolosh to blow our minor gripes into divides of major proportion.

I was stuck in the dark corners of my mind until the world, in the form of a twenty-one-year-old college senior, crashed through my bathroom window in the middle of a February Sunday.

While the attack had caused a lot of my problems, I was clear that they hadn't started there. I didn't know how, or even if, healing was possible. But I knew I had to do something. I had to right my relationship with myself. My physical wounds had been extremely painful, but they were nothing compared to the psychological agony I was in now.

If I wanted others to treat me better, I needed to start treating myself better. I came to see that we can only receive what we give to ourselves.

When I had done the earlier work on forgiveness, almost always, the person who was hardest to forgive was myself. The person hardest to feel compassion, kindness and love toward was myself.

Looking for answers that could explain the attack from a spiritual perspective, I found solace in the Huna worldview of the Ancient Hawaiians, who believed that we come into this world to heal the wounds and clean up the unfinished business of our past—our own, as well as our ancestors'. The more we clean up and heal, the closer we come to liberation and oneness with our creator.

Our resistance and unwillingness to explore discomfort provide a safe haven for the very things we are trying to avoid. By refusing to bring our unresolved emotions to the surface, we breathe life into the Tokolosh, the proverbial zombie, rooted in the dead past.

Instead, Huna wisdom, like Zen and many other traditions, including modern psychology, advises this: when life presents a difficulty, whether it be a financial hardship, an illness, or a conflict with a co-worker, the first step is to work through resistance and accept what is, instead of pushing it away or sweeping it under the rug.

Recognizing that "life" extends far beyond our conscious awareness in physical form, the underlying tenet of Huna practice is complete responsibility for your own life and whatever it is that comes up for you—without attaching shame, blame or guilt.

When you have been a victim of a violent crime, accepting responsibility is not an easy thing to do, until you realize that blame and responsibility are not the same thing. Taking responsibility gives us control. You can blame and punish others for what has happened to you until the end of time, but it won't change your situation until you begin to make the change inside of you.

Part 4: Fall Harvest

Missing Links

One night, in the beginning of September, I woke up at 3:33 AM with the thought that I needed to start *A Course in Miracles*. The book had been on my bookshelf wrapped in cellophane for years, maybe decades, and I had never opened it.

I got the dark blue book off the shelf, tore off the plastic wrapper and read the summary introduction:

" . . . The course does not aim at teaching the meaning of love, for that is beyond what can be taught. It does aim, however, at removing the blocks to the awareness of love's presence, which is your natural inheritance. The opposite of love is fear, but what is all-encompassing can have no opposite."

I didn't know a great deal about the premise of the teachings but the "pull" to learn more was strong—even urgent. The book was voluminous and though it said it was "self-study," I was skeptical. I looked on the internet for classes near me and found nothing.

The next Sunday I was on my way to my Zen group when I suddenly got the idea to go to the Melbourne Unity Church instead. I'd never been there, but I'd driven by it dozens of times, so I went to check it out. During the service, they announced a new *Course in Miracles* class beginning the following week—on the only open night in my schedule.

Though *A Course in Miracles* was new to me, the philosophy behind it was not, and the ideas mostly fit into my existing world view. However, as I dug into the workbook, I found that the exercises helped me integrate aspirations into my life in a practical way that I had never experienced before. It also provided some of the missing links I needed to make my healing complete.

Until then, I hadn't truly understood the relationship between fear and love. At the time, though I was making progress in my overall state and accepting the circumstances of my life, I was still struggling with my own feelings of guilt and unworthiness. I didn't realize that I wasn't alone in these types of feelings.

My healing work was not a straight line to bliss. I dived deeply into working through the ocean of guilt, both conscious and unconscious, that I'd been accumulating since birth. And that is never easy.

In the *Course*, guilt is a broader concept than what we usually interpret the word to mean. In fact, *A Course in Miracles* attributes all human problems to some form of guilt, which, for most people, is unconscious. Our biblical interpretations and misunderstanding of our relationship with God, woven into our collective consciousness, feed these false ideas.

Typically, we think about guilt as it relates to

something we DID but in the *Course*, guilt is connected more to WHO we are. It could express itself as a feeling that something is "wrong" with you, that you are "not enough," or that you don't "deserve to be alive."

Perhaps you can look at your life—or that of a loved one—and see how the projection of guilt/unworthiness has manifested.   And perhaps when you look at those manifestations, the relationship between cause and effect may be interchangeable.

In my case, as the youngest child by four-plus years, I was treated differently than my older sisters. Naturally my sisters were envious and picked on me like most older siblings do to their younger kin. The fact that they were adopted was a constant point of contention and I came to believe that my birth was to blame for the lack of love my sisters felt. Whenever they were scolded, punished or disciplined—which was often—my young heart went through a shredder. I knew it had to be my fault.

When my two closest sisters died from illness, both in their forties, it ripped open the old scars. I did not deal with the psychological trauma then, but turned away, letting it fester in the darkest corners of my being.

At that point, I could speak at length about why and how guilt, fear and anger sabotage us and keep us stuck—or how destructive feelings of unworthiness were. But until I began studying the *Course*, I didn't know how to reconcile the ideas in a universal way that could absolve all of it. The *Course* was my missing link.

Now, thanks to the deeper understanding it provided, I had another opportunity to heal those childhood wounds, brought into the light once again with the attempted suicide of my estranged sister. I saw how the symbiotic relationships between shame, guilt and unworthiness solidified the behavior patterns that had sabotaged my happiness. But I learned that the more gently I behaved toward myself, the kinder the world became toward me.

Using all the resources at my disposal, I focused on self-healing, self-love and building back my faith. After three months of good daily habits that included long walks, meditation, faithful application of the ancient Hawaiian and Tibetan remedies, yoga, daily lessons from *A Course in Miracles*, and drastic reduction of alcohol consumption, I was renewed. I had found my cowboy suit and though I was a lot older and wiser, it still fit.

Surrender

A hurricane came through in October, taking down my fence, and causing me to cancel another business launch. Was the Universe trying to tell me something?

Money was tight and the presidential elections worrisome, but despite outer circumstances, inwardly I was feeling happy and whole again. Fulfilling my promise of only focusing on what I could control or influence, I worked hard for my presidential candidate going into November. She lost. Shocked, I found myself exhausted from the emotional rollercoaster of the past year, ready to surrender. What other surprises could possibly be in store?

Looking at my calendar, I was somewhat taken aback to see that the meeting I'd requested with my attacker, months prior, was scheduled for the coming Friday, November 11th.

Did I even want that now?

All my friends thought that a face-to-face confrontation with my attacker was a terrible idea. There were so many things that could go wrong, they cautioned. I was doing well now and they worried that the meeting had the potential to bring back the Tokolosh.

I briefly considered cancelling the meeting. The reasons for it no longer seemed important. I was comfortable letting the judicial system take care of his punishment and moving forward with my life the best way I could.

But I felt strong and truly wanted to let go of whatever anger and resentment remained in my heart. I reasoned that the meeting would bring closure and help put the whole terrifying experience behind me. So, I decided to go ahead with it, determined not to be afraid.

Day of Reckoning

The day I would have the opportunity to confront my attacker arrived. I had been so obsessed with the election that I hadn't given any thought to what I would say when I saw him. But now it was D-Day and my mind was swirling with unanswerable questions.

Will an apology satisfy the indignation I still feel?

In my heart, I had "sort of" forgiven him, but I still struggled with the unfairness of it all. I wanted deeply to be okay with what had happened. But I still wanted "justice." I'd lost so much time, my business was in shambles, and I was physically still somewhat impaired. Could I ever get over this final hurdle?

And if I do, and I agree to a reduced sentence. . .what if in twenty years from now, he kills someone?

I gathered the digital photos I had taken with my phone on the days following the incident and put them in an album in my iPad. It seemed important for the young man to see how brutal his actions had been. Perhaps it could prevent moral hazard in the future.

I wondered whether his parents would be there, and if I should have asked someone to go with me for support.

Is this a mistake? Should I have cancelled the whole thing? How will I feel when I see him? Will I panic? Will it trigger the terror I felt?

"Too late to worry about that now!" I told myself as I picked up my keys and headed out the door.

It was a beautiful, partly cloudy Florida morning with temperatures in the mid-seventies. I wanted to arrive before the other side did, so I left early and took the scenic route. Driving along the river, I talked to God out loud, laying out my feelings, my desires and concerns.

After a while, I narrowed my request down to this: "Show me what I need to see, guide me in my actions, thoughts and words. Please clear my mind of judgment and preconception. Show me what is right and true because obviously, I don't know."

Feeling my heart murmuring in my chest, I worried that I was headed for a heart attack and whether seeing a cardiologist would make it more difficult to get insurance in the future.

I did my best to apply the Zen practice of relaxing into what I was experiencing without critique. I felt the resistance in my body and the impulse to distract myself. "Stay, Stay…," I told myself, and took a few deep breaths. Eventually, acceptance washed over me like a cool, soft wave on a warm summer day.

"I can do this," I said confidently.

Midway between my house and the office, I got a call from my lawyer's assistant. Mr. Johnson had arrived early.

His father and lawyer were with him.

Darn! My peaceful acceptance from just a few moments before evaporated. *I wanted to get there first!*

Worrying that I would be at a disadvantage walking into a room where my opponents were already comfortable, I asked the legal assistant to put them somewhere else until I got settled in the conference room.

My mind began to spin again but this time I smiled because I noticed it BEFORE it hooked me.

"Choose again, Mandy!" I told myself. Gently, I consciously moved my attention to the big, open blue sky, the puffy white clouds, and the calm, quiet river to my right. Then I went back to my conversation with God.

Divine Intervention

B onnie, the legal assistant, set me up in the conference room. I wasn't surprised that my lawyer didn't think this meeting worthy of his time, but I was starting to feel alone and vulnerable.

I reminded myself that I wasn't truly alone and that meeting would be a lot more difficult for the assailant than me. If this didn't go well, with one word from me, the State Attorney could be making a case for him to spend life in prison.

A few weeks prior, the District Attorney called me to get my thoughts on appropriate sentencing.

"On the one hand," I told her, "he is so young! I don't want his entire life to be ruined. If he goes to a prison with other felons, he may not survive. And if he does, he will likely become a hardened criminal."

"Well, he did something really bad," she said.

"Yes, but if what his lawyer says is true, it was his first offense. And he was under the influence of LSD, not in his right mind."

"That is still not an excuse for what he did," she reminded me.

"The thing that concerns me is that I would be complicit if he commits another crime. If he gets off too leniently, how will he learn? There needs to be some punishment."

"Well," she said, "let's look at each count one at a time."

We went over each felony count that he was charged with, and his lawyer's requests in each case. We agreed that what the lawyer was asking for, on Ken's behalf, was ridiculous. That no way could we agree to a plea that allowed the assailant to serve probation, without jail time. And we agreed that the request for "withholding of adjudication" was absurd and not a point of negotiation.

In Florida, withholding of adjudication allows a person to potentially end up with a clean record. If the person meets the court requirements, after they have served probation, they have no guilty conviction on their record.

"Are you okay?" Bonnie asked. "Shall I get them?"

"Sure," I said.

As soon as she left the room, I turned my eyes upward and imagined turning the meeting over to Higher Intelligence.

The door opened. I took a deep breath.

Three men in suits, each bearing gifts, filed into the room. Ken was in front, dressed in a grey suit, holding a French pastry box. His father followed with a big vase of red roses, and at the back of the line, their attorney carried a vase of yellow roses.

I thanked them and shook hands with Ken's attorney and his dad. The two older men were now opposite me on the other side of the conference table. Ken walked to the head of the table. He was now standing next to me, immediately to my left.

As we stood around the table, completing the introductions, I began to feel a bit lightheaded. I put my hand on the conference table to steady myself and a sense of calmness washed over me.

I don't know that words are sufficient to describe what happened next: It was like stepping through a time warp and having the barriers that separate us from one another fall away.

It was as if I had plugged into a socket that gave me access to a world that is always there but cannot be seen with our physical eyes. A current of eternity—devoid of separation.

I became aware of thoughts and feelings that seemed to be those of the other people in the room, as if I was experiencing their senses through my body.

I could feel the deep bond between father and son. Pride buried by distress, shame and guilt. Expectations trapped between hope and fear of disappointment.

I have no idea how long that experience lasted. Or how it might have looked from the other side of the table. Suddenly I became aware that everyone was looking at me, as if expecting me to say something.

I looked at Ken. "You don't look nearly as scary as

you did last time I saw you," I blurted out, trying to lighten things up.

Ken's hands started to tremble. I could feel him starting to break.

"I am sorry," he said. He shook visibly.

Instinctively I put my arms around him to give him a hug. He began to weep. Like a mother consoling a child, I held him as he sobbed into my shoulder.

As we stood there, Ken crying into my shoulder and me holding and comforting him, the whole world seemed to shift. Through the sea of human emotion, I could see the innate goodness of Ken and his father, shining like beacons of light.

Then the feelings receded and I was aware of a sense of pure being.   No fear, no shame, no judgment, no guilt. All that was left was Oneness. All I could feel was Love.

"I forgive you . . . God forgives you . . .," I whispered, patting my attacker's back as he clung to me, tears streaming down his cheeks. "It's going to be okay. I promise."

Eventually we sat down and talked about what happened. I showed them the pictures. They told me about their lives. Except for the lawyer making sure to get his talking points in, it felt like a reunion of long-lost friends.

I had turned the situation over to God. He had delivered beyond my wildest expectations.

Dear Reader:

Before I continue with my story, I invite you to use this page for yours.

If it feels right, rest here for a moment to breathe and consider a place in your life where you feel stuck.

What if you could let go of your ideas about how things "should be" in this area? What might be possible if you just surrendered control? What could happen if you asked higher intelligence for guidance—even if you don't truly believe in such a thing?

If you could, would you? Why not try it now?

M

Afterglow

For weeks after my Veteran's Day experience, I felt like I was in a waking dream of love consciousness. My health spontaneously improved, and except for some achiness in my right arm and wrist, I was back to my vibrant self again. As corny and unlikely as it sounds—even to me—it was like being in love, except in this case, my devotion was universal. My heart was completely open and I was motivated to right all my relationships.

As I developed more self-awareness, I realized that I had been carrying all sorts of grudges against people: the friend who revealed a confidence I had shared; the business associate who "stole" a client; the employee who disappointed; the client who misdirected his anger toward me. I could go on. I had loads of baggage I'd been carrying around for years.

If I can forgive my attacker, surely, I can let go of these grievances!

With a strong desire to let things go, I quickly and easily disposed of most of them using an exercise that I had used in the corporate world to help people develop emotional flexibility, one of the most important soft skills needed for sales and leadership.

Having emotional flexibility simply means that you can look at a situation from various points of view, and by doing so, you're able to achieve a more enlightened perspective, understanding how the situation affects all the people involved.

You begin by looking at a situation that involves at least one other person. First, you replay the experience in your mind's eye from your own point of view, allowing the scene to unfold just as you experienced it when it actually happened, noticing your feelings.

Next, you imagine stepping out of yourself and witnessing the same situation from an observer's point of view. This observer has no stake in the situation that transpired and you simply witness the same set of events from a completely objective, unemotional point of view, taking note of what you notice.

The third step is to imagine the events play out, but this time you see it from the other person's point of view, doing your best to see what they saw, hear what they heard, feel what they felt.

Finally, you can imagine yourself in the center of the galaxy with access to infinite wisdom and the knowledge of all time and space, looking down at the tiny blue rotating ball we call the earth, watching the same event play out from that perspective.

It is a powerful and simple exercise. If you really engage in this process, you will gain remarkable insights from everyday interactions that may have triggered you in the past. Most of the time you realize that people's actions are often a result of carelessness, misunderstanding, or haste.

Looking at the behaviors that angered me, I noticed they were often actions I could accuse myself of, many times over. And as I shed petty grievances and resentment, I felt more connected and at peace. At the same time, I became more tuned in to the suffering of other people.

My righteousness about the attack dissolved and I thought more about Ken's safety and future. After meeting him, I knew he would never make it in prison with hardened criminals. There had been enough suffering. No punishment would reverse the pain of the past. I wanted only good to come out of what had happened.

I made numerous efforts to contact the District Attorney to tell her about my change of heart: I didn't want him to go to prison. I left long voicemail messages and followed up with emails detailing my wishes for how the case should proceed. In the past, she had always returned my calls promptly, but not now. Now there was only silence.

After the November meeting, I was in frequent email contact with Ken's dad. Naturally they worried. I worried too.

Days passed, then weeks. Nothing. I sent another email. Nothing. I called again.

"I am really hoping we can get this wrapped up before Christmas," I said to her voicemail, trying to create a sense of urgency.

Was she listening? I didn't know, so I kept trying.

Christmas came and went as Ken's future swung uncertainly in the wind.

Part 5: Light Returns

Sacred Relationships

Right after Christmas, my mother drove up from Miami to visit for two weeks. We made a daily ritual of walking over the Indian River bridge at sunrise, playing Scrabble and indulging in chocolate-dipped Danish butter cookies with tea.

Relaxed, comfortable and enjoying our time together, we cleaned out my garage, planted potted poinsettias in the backyard and discussed world events. It was the kind of loving mother-daughter relationship we had always wanted but never had.

The shift in our relationship was remarkable, and I came to see what a gift it is to have my mother around. I decided to overlook the things that used to hook me. Instead of getting triggered when she interrupted my morning meditation practice, I invited her to join me, guiding both of us into a state of relaxed, open-hearted awareness.

When habit kicked in, and I found myself caught in the net of combat, I relaxed and let go. Then I forgave myself and chose again. My new attitude allowed her to relax and be less defensive.

Now I see that I am blessed every day with the sacred

opportunity to give my mother the life she always wanted. That is not to say that it is always easy for us or between us. Our relationship may never be perfect but it has certainly progressed. Of all the accomplishments I have had in my life, this is the one I am most proud of. If this realization was the only good thing to come out of the attack, all that pain, suffering and heartache would truly have been worth it.

Making Things Right with Mr. Right

Listening to the audio version of *A Course in Miracles*, I made my way across the state to Lovers Key, an exquisite nature preserve near Fort Myers Beach. Mr. Right and I had spent our first weekend away together there.

A year had passed since the attack, and he invited me to the island to spend a few days with him. After finding out about the assault, he was terribly upset and did whatever he could to help me.

It seemed to me that I had a blind spot. Over the past three years I often wondered what I had done to cause him to want to break up a great relationship. My imaginings of why things ended encompassed a wide range of possibilities. Most of them aimed at me feeling unworthy and undeserving.

Whatever it was, I wanted to know.

"I'm writing a book," I told him. "If I come, I'll want to spend some time there writing."

"That's great," he said. "Of course."

"I also want to talk about us. I want to understand

what happened."

He agreed.

Would he finally tell me the truth about why he did what he did?

As I crossed over the bridge to the condo he had rented, I realized that he, like the rest of us, was driven by unconscious impulses that most people don't understand. He too is a magician transforming his outer circumstances to reflect his inner world. Even if he could "explain" what had happened, it would just be an interpretation of his understanding. And, perception is not truth. It is just an opinion.

Suddenly I realized that finding out what had happened to us was not important—nor the reason I had come. I knew that at some level he felt guilty, and that somehow the tumult of the past year was his fault.

Admittedly, in the early days after the assault, there was a part of me that blamed him for the situation I found myself in. In those days, I blamed everyone. Now I knew better. I wanted to assure him that what had happened was not his fault. The past was over and there was nothing to forgive.

It was clear: my work now was to release him, to release both of us from the chains of guilt and regret.

As we walked the white sandy shores, we shared our most intimate thoughts. Our love and affection for one another was never stronger. But there was no part of me that wanted us to be any more than the good friends we had become.

I never found out what the straw was that broke our relationship. But if I had to guess, I would say it was the Tokolosh. What else but fear causes us to put up walls, shut down, separate, doubt, or get angry?

As I began my four-hour journey home, I realized that however unreal the Tokolosh was, it was nevertheless a part of me, a part of Mr. Right, a part of us all. Left untethered, it creates conflict, confusion and paralysis. But resisting it, and pushing it into a dark corner, had never worked either. The only solution was to tame it and bring it into the light.

Finally, I was ready to take it on.

I invited the fearful part of me to be my companion on the long drive back to Melbourne. As was the Ancient Huna practice, I thanked the Tokolosh for showing up and offered my love and appreciation. I forgave it for the angst I thought it caused me and asked its forgiveness for having pushed it away in the past, without listening to what it had to say.

If, in fact, the Huna were right about every adversity being a gift that can bring you closer to your creator, the Tokolosh had, indeed, brought me many gifts.

As I approached my exit I turned my audio book back on, and I heard as if on cue:

"As you forgive him, you restore to truth what was denied by both of you. And you will see forgiveness where you have given it."

"Abracadabra you are free!" I said out loud, pulling

into my driveway. Looking through the eyes of love, I had tamed the Tokolosh. For today, at least, we were free and at peace.

My Personal Batman

Despite the twenty-plus-year age gap, Ken and I had plenty to talk about as we sat at the dining room table, eating the delicious salmon dinner I had prepared. He showed me a short video of a music contest he had just won, and we shared our thoughts about what was happening in the world and in our lives. It was just the kind of conversation you would want to have with your twenty-two-year-old son.

Never having had my own children, it was heartwarming to feel so close and connected to this bright, talented, sensitive college graduate.

As we chatted about his budding music career and how he could increase his social media presence, I couldn't help noticing that he was sitting on the very chair he had used thirteen months earlier to break my arm. It was hard to believe that this sweet man was the same person who had attacked me in a drug-induced rage.

The last time he visited, a young friend of his had just committed suicide. We talked about the challenges of young people, the dangers of drugs and peer pressure, two subjects whose risks we were both now expert in.

"Perhaps we could speak as a duo?" I suggested lightheartedly.

He was more a musician than a speaker, so I suggested he write a song.

"No," he said. "I want to do an album."

"Of course you do!" I laughed, loving his confidence that everything is possible.

Our connection was warm and caring with just enough arrogance and attitude from him for me to know that he was completely authentic. The fact that we could have a relationship at all was quite remarkable.

In mid-January, I had gotten my answer in the form of an email. The District Attorney sent me a copy of their plea offer to approve. It was exactly what I asked for. Exactly what the lawyer had petitioned for. I asked for only one change: that the "no contact clause" be removed.

After the hearing, I received a text from Ken that said,

"Hello Mandy!!! This is Ken Johnson. I cannot thank you enough for your compassion and understanding. I can guarantee that I will make a positive difference in the world and help others from my experiences.

Warren Buffett said, 'We learn from mistakes, but they don't have to be yours,' so I will do my best to help others follow a path of righteousness. Please, please, please let me know if there is anything you need or would like from me. Consider me your personal batman, shine the light and unless something is truly preventing me from being there, I will be there.

Thank you so much again."

Epilogue

As I write this last chapter, I am sitting on my sofa, in the same spot in my family room where I spent the first days and nights after my attack. I am hunkered down, waiting for the onslaught of Hurricane Irma, the largest hurricane to be recorded, now a Category Four.

The hype and hysteria preceding this storm have been extraordinary and I wonder if this kind of fear and panic may be at least as dangerous as the wrathful side of Nature herself. Certainly, that has been my personal experience.

"Do you think we will be okay?" my mother asks, nervously, watching the endless news coverage of the gigantic storm's approach.

I'd insisted she come up from Miami and stay with me to ride out what I was calling "Irma-geddon." I knew, at the very least, we would lose power and I didn't want her stranded, alone and afraid.

"Let's hope so," said Beth, a friend who lived in a mandatory evacuation zone.

I opened my house to the many friends I've cultivated in the area over the past year, people who needed a safehouse for the storm, and she was the only one who took me up on the offer.

"We are going to be fine, ladies," I said. "Just fine. "

"You would think by now the government would have developed a weapon to send into the clouds and break up these storms," my mom said, horrified at the TV images of Irma barreling toward us, carving a deadly path of destruction, demolishing everything in her way.

"I think what we need is to figure out how we can live in harmony with Nature. Not how to destroy it. We have done enough of that," I said, adding, "I promise. We will be fine."

I am completely calm and unafraid. Not because I know what the outcome of the storm will be, but because there is an amazing sense of freedom that comes from surviving the storms of life—if you are willing to let go and stop trying to control what is not within your power to control, if you are open to allowing unimagined possibilities to unfold.

Many of us operate under the assumption that we can control what happens around us—even nature. We get up in the morning planning, manipulating, scheming about how we can make things turn out the way we think they should. And despite the fact that things SELDOM go exactly as planned, we still wake up the next morning, and the one after that, thinking the same way.

It is as if there is a Cosmic Joker who sprinkles stardust over us when we sleep, so we forget our experience and repeat the same thing all over again. It seems insane, but many of us keep doing it anyway.

Over the years, I have been repeatedly surprised by very accomplished people in business, politics, the arts and sciences, who attribute their success to "accident," "luck," or being in the right place at the right time. Now I am beginning to understand their secret.

I don't mean to imply that those people didn't work hard or are undeserving. What I mean is that they took what life presented to them and made something of it. They didn't have some grand scheme that they were manifesting. Instead, they approached their work in an open-hearted way that allowed them to see the gifts Life offered, leaving the grand design to a force greater than themselves.

Because our brains are wired to bring to our attention the information that it believes we WANT to see, most of us walk around with invisible blinders on, obsessing about our uninspired goals, oblivious to the potential of the moment we are in.

A few hours ago, I sat down to "come up with" a final chapter to close out my story. Having surrendered to the moment, I now see that the ending is writing itself. (If I can just submit and allow it to happen.)

Out of the corner of my eye I see my cell phone light up with a text message. It is Ken, wanting to make sure I am safe. A few months ago, he got a great job and moved out of state. Before he was hired, his new employer, aware of what had transpired, called me, seeking assurance that they were making the right decision in hiring him. I wanted nothing more than for him to be successful, and earnestly encouraged them to give him a chance.

On my phone, I have several other messages: Mr. Right offered me cautious, solid advice; my dear friend Lynn offered assistance if needed; Adrienne, who was finally released from the specialty burn unit she was a patient in for almost a year, sent a message of prayer; and my oldest sister, Mary-Anne, summoned the force that brought us together as sisters-in-spirit again. The same force that healed my heart and repaired my relationships.

What is that power, that force?

I like to call it Love.

In Sanskrit, there are 96 words for love. Ancient Persian has 80, Greek three, and English only one. In English, we use the same word for how we feel about a spouse, parents, a friend, our children, when our hormones are raging, or our devotion to God.

One of my favorite teachers, Adyashanti, speaks of "Redemptive Love," which he describes as a Grace, a gift, that doesn't have to be earned or justified in any way, a deep, fundamental aspect of our own being that is available to us whenever we call upon its presence.

Fear, shame, unworthiness and guilt proliferate in secret, hiding that unshakable, immovable essence inside of you, inside of us all. But when we take the Tokolosh into light and look at it for what it truly is, we realize that most of what we are afraid of is not real and not present, but instead the product of our overactive imaginations conjuring up frightful scenarios that will probably never happen.

We realize that perception is not reality, and to empower ourselves, all we need do is accept what is—and allow the gift of the moment to reveal itself. Then, quite automatically, we become aware of possibilities we may never have considered before.

"Imagine," Adyashanti says, "Instead of the old worn out story of unworthiness and insufficiency, that almost all of us have inherited . . . that the reason you are here is to redeem yourself to wholeness. Imagine that your existence is in no way a mistake. That you are here ... as an act of Love . . . to redeem all the painful places in your being."—*Healing the Core Wound of Unworthiness: The Gift of Redemptive Love*

It is this kind of Love I hope my experience will inspire you to seek: the kind that has literally and figuratively healed my heart as well as my relationships with others. By healing ourselves, we help to heal the world.

I feel so blessed to be the beneficiary of this story. Thank you for allowing me to share it with you.

Part 6: Mandy's Mind Tools and Resources

For guided audios of these exercises, please visit
MindToSucceed.com

Awakening Awareness

Conscious Awareness is the faculty that makes all other healing states possible because it allows us to know and experience the present moment, see where we are stuck, what is happening, and what is called for. By quieting our minds, we get in touch with a deeper part of ourselves that is always present when we are present to it.

Most of us fill our lives with constant busyness and distraction, and we avoid dealing with feelings we find difficult or unpleasant. When we don't take care of our emotional, mental and spiritual hygiene, those issues often manifest into more serious problems. Conscious Awareness is a state of clarity and insight that is naturally available to us when we clear ourselves of mental clutter and let go of our everyday-thinking-mind. Awareness enables us to observe what is truly present—without judgment, critique or the need to control the outcome.

Cultivating Awareness Exercise

From my perspective, a regular meditation practice is the best way to cultivate awareness on an ongoing basis. In this exercise, there is nothing to accomplish or achieve. The purpose is to experience the present moment detached from your thoughts with curiosity and openness. To do that, you will need to put aside the identity you have with your problem-solving, "knowing" mind. This open, non-judgmental perspective is known as "beginners mind," a deeper state of attention, receptivity and peace.

- Make sure you are in a quiet place where you won't be disturbed or distracted.

- Ideally set aside twenty minutes, but even five or ten minutes will be helpful.

- Do not struggle or strive to achieve anything. Simply approach this exercise with curiosity.

- We build awareness by being quiet inside and noticing what is truly happening within us and around us—outside of our thoughts. Instead of striving to solve problems or make things happen a certain way, relax and allow yourself a little vacation from thinking.

- It is unlikely that you will stop thinking. What you want to do is disengage your awareness from that part of you so that you can notice that your thoughts are just thoughts. Notice them as you would notice autumn leaves falling from a tree. They are not you. You can choose to stop paying attention to them. You can choose to be quiet as they drift away.

- Be compassionate with yourself. Whenever you

become aware that you are being carried away by your thoughts, forgive yourself and make a conscious decision to come back to concentrating on your breath again. Do this no matter how many times it happens. The fact that you are catching yourself getting "hooked" by thought means that you are cultivating awareness.

- Remember that there is nothing to make happen. You are simply building your ability to unhook from the craziness of your mind, so that you can get in touch with what else is present.

There is no right or wrong way to consciously experience Awareness. The following steps are simply a guide:

1. Sit comfortably and settle in for a few moments, focusing on your breath going in and out of your belly. Be quiet even if your mind seems unruly.
2. Most people find it easier to close their eyes to shut out distraction, but you can also practice with your eyes open by fixing your gaze on an object or spot in front of you.
3. Allow yourself to become aware of your thoughts. Be curious, watching, aware that you are not them—no more than you are autumn leaves. No matter how neurotic your thoughts get, remain still, observe, be curious and let them pass. Don't judge, analyze or get carried away by them. Observe for a few minutes as

you breathe in and out.

4. It is natural to get hooked by a thought and let several minutes pass before you realize it. If that happens, be gentle with yourself and bring yourself back to your breath.

5. Once you feel comfortable with separating yourself from your thoughts and have successfully unattached yourself from your thinking a few times, ask yourself: *Who is it that is doing the thinking?* There is no need to answer this question with logic, just be present for whatever you are sensing. Observe. Don't judge. Just notice what you notice. *If you are not your thoughts, who is here?* Again, be still, curious and open.

6. Notice what you are feeling. *Where are you feeling that feeling? What are the qualities (texture / temperature / sensation) of that feeling?* Sit with the sensation a few moments and avoid getting into the narrative about those feelings. *What is under that feeling?*

7. *What else is here?*

8. *If there are no thoughts to think, no problems to solve, what is here?* Feel what you feel; notice what you notice. Simply allow yourself to be aware of your awareness.

9. Notice your awareness INSIDE your body.

10. Notice your awareness BEYOND the edges of your body—in front, behind, to the left and to the right, above and below. *How far does it extend? What do you sense? What else do you notice?*

11. Bring your attention back to the stillness of your

breath for a few moments before coming out, giving thanks for these moments of peace and awareness.

Emotional Flexibility Exercises
Part I: Perceptual Positions

This exercise helps you harmonize and accept situations in your life by giving you the benefit of a more complete view of what took place.

There are many different ways to see and remember things. For example, tonight you can look back on your day and recall it the way it looked through your own eyes, or you could see it as if you were an observer watching yourself going about the day. Let's say you had an argument with a co-worker. You could see that argument playing out in those two ways. Or you could recall the argument, imagining it through your co-worker's eyes.

If we recall a situation through our own eyes, we tend to be more emotional; through Observer eyes, we are typically more objective, and when we imagine the situation through the eyes of the Other person, we tend to be more empathetic. Seeing things cleanly from different perspectives can make it easier to let go of grievances, feel more at peace and find common ground.

By changing your perceptual position, your feelings about the incident naturally adapt. You could also imagine looking at the situation from 10,000 feet, or from the center of the galaxy where you can imagine seeing the incident from the perspective of divine wisdom, or divine love. That really changes it!

All perspectives have advantages and disadvantages. The ability to move between perceptual positions at will gives you access to a deeper, more rounded understanding of events. With practice, you can begin to use this valuable skill automatically to balance your insights and get a wiser, more holistic perspective of life.

This technique is provided for resolving normal disagreements or grudges that involve another person. (It is not intended for trauma cases without the guidance of a trained professional.)

1. Choose an incident that you WANT to feel better about. The incident should be one that involves another person and is easy to recall. (Note: Your feelings won't change unless you desire it.)

2. Step into the experience again. Be there. View the scene from the perspective of your own eyes, in your body, feeling your "own" feelings, looking at the scene but unable to see your own face. *Note your experience of "Self" Position.*

3. Step out, zoom away and be detached as if you are watching yourself and the entire scene safely from a distance. You can "see" yourself over there, what your face looks like, how you walk, who you are

interacting with, the surroundings etc. *What is your experience of the situation as an Observer?*

4. Now imagine for a moment that you can step into the body of the other person in this situation. View the scene as if you are the other person, through their eyes, with their feelings, history and experience. It may feel like you are making it up and that is okay. *What is your experience of the situation as the "Other" person?* If this feels too difficult for you, imagine seeing the situation through the eyes of someone who loves that "Other" person such as the "Other" person's parent or child. *What is different?*

5. To get an even broader perspective, imagine zooming out further to the center of the galaxy, from a viewpoint of infinite wisdom and all time and space. *What is different?*

6. Look at the situation again from your own perspective. *What healing realizations are coming to you now that you have had the benefit of all these perspectives?*

Emotional Flexibility Exercises
Part II: Letting Go

If you have practiced the **Perceptual Positions Exercise**, still feel a grudge AND you really want to let it go, practice this exercise:

1. Quiet your mind and concentrate on your breathing for a few minutes.
2. Bring to mind the incident (or person) that you want to let go of.
3. Gently put your attention onto it. What is the feeling? Notice where it is located, its size, its shape and how it feels. DO NOT GET INTO THE STORY.
4. Stay focused on the sensations of the feeling. Breathe into the sensations for a few moments and notice any shifts in location, size, shape and quality. Thoughts or your story about your feelings only feed and strengthen the pain, like throwing wood into a fire. When thoughts arise, simply allow them to pass and gently bring your attention back to the raw sensation.
5. When you have fully experienced the feeling, and are

ready to release it, ask:

- *Could I let this feeling go?* If yes, ask:
- *Would I?* If yes, ask:
- *When?*

6. Repeat the sequence, answering the questions each time until you feel a shift and can no longer access the feeling.

7. If you were unable to get to "yes" in Step 5, work with the **Forgiveness: Building Desire Exercise** to build your willingness to let go.

Fear: Stepping into the Unknown Visualization

If you are hesitating about doing something you need to do because you fear what "could happen," this exercise can help you take the next step by bringing the unknown into the familiar.

1. Identify the situation you want to resolve.
2. When you think about taking "the next step," what is it that you afraid of? (Be specific.)
3. Separate out what is real (things you know for sure and have evidence of) vs. what you are imagining (e.g. mind reading, what "could" happen, etc.).
4. What would you prefer to have happen in this scenario?
5. Given what you know about the situation and taking "all realities into account," (e.g. I knew that the window was broken when I was searching for Advil) how would the best-case scenario play out?
6. What do you want to have happen if this exercise is successful? What will you see, hear and feel?

7. Why is the above important to you?   What is important about *that*?

8. Close your eyes and create a picture in your mind of a positive scenario playing out, considering all the realities you know about the situation. Notice any place in the visualization where you still feel resistance or fear. Acknowledge those feelings and zoom in to get clear about what is real vs. what is imagined.

9. See yourself successfully taking the next baby step and feel how good it feels.

10. Open your eyes. Take some action toward the goal now—even if it is a tiny step.

Forgiveness: Building Desire

1. Get into a relaxed state and spend a few moments focused on your breath: nice slow deep breaths. Try to maintain slow rhythmic breathing throughout the process. If your mind wanders, bring your attention back to your breath for a minute, then return to the place in the exercise where you got distracted.

2. Think of a person that you are having difficulty forgiving and spend a few moments tuned into the feelings you feel toward that person, noticing where in your body you feel those feelings and the qualities of the sensations. Your goal is to STAY with the feeling and work through resistance.

3. Think about someone or something you feel unconditional love/friendliness toward. It could be a child, pet, or even someone from your past. Notice where in your body you feel those feelings of love and notice the qualities of the sensations. Really allow yourself to enjoy those feelings.

4. Imagine how great it would be to feel this type of open-heartedness more often.

5. Compare those feelings to the feelings of resentment.

Given the choice, which feelings would you rather have?

6. To expand the feeling of open-heartedness, imagine the person, pet or thing you thought about earlier to generate good feelings, and send her/him loving-kindness and compassion and feel them sending rays of unconditional love back to you. Enjoy the sending and receiving for a few moments.

7. Start adding people you know into your visualizations, sending love to them and imagining them sending love back to you. Begin with people you know who are easier to love, and work on expanding it to people you are neutral toward. It is natural to feel resistance. Don't worry if it is hard for you to keep connected to those loving feelings. Your intention is what counts. Make believe you can feel it.

8. Eventually work on expanding those feelings to people you don't know, and then to those you don't like or have disagreements with.

9. Expand those feelings to people who have hurt you in a small, unintentional way, sending them a wish that they be happy and free from suffering. Notice how good it feels to send love or compassion to people. Notice how different this feels from anger and resentment. *Imagine how it would feel to have this level of friendliness toward all beings.*

10. When you are ready, you can work with the harder cases, using this technique or some of the other techniques offered here.

Huna Exercise

Huna Practice Principles

1. "Problems" are an opportunity to "clean" up our past (our own as well as that of our ancestors.) Instead of resisting problems, we can embrace them, grateful for the healing opportunity.
2. In order to clean and resolve difficulties, we need to accept responsibility for them.
3. Responsibility and blame are not the same thing. Why those problems occurred, or who is "at fault," are not of concern. Our job is simply to heal and clean.
4. Every time you "clean" something up, the closer you get to Love and oneness with the creator.

These steps are an example of how to apply the above principles:

1. **Accept responsibility**: "I accept whatever is it in ME that is causing or contributing to this situation." *Once we accept responsibility for what is happening to us, we then have the power to change it. When we blame others for our*

troubles we give our power to them.

2. **Appreciate:** "Thank you for this opportunity to clean this up."

3. **Apologize:** "I am sorry for whatever it is in me that is contributing to this issue."

4. **Choose to let it go:** "I forgive and release whatever it is in me that is creating this."

5. **Affirm:** "I love you."

If you are using this technique to harmonize a relationship with another person (or a part of yourself), after a few moments imagine them mirroring the above back to you, accepting, appreciating, apologizing, choosing to let go and affirming their love for you.

Love in this context is love in the global sense, not to be confused with romantic love.

Meditation

There are many different meditation methods. One is not necessarily better than another; they are just different. Each has pros and cons. People who meditate tend to think that THEIR form of practice is the best! So, my advice is to pick one method and get started. They are all beneficial to mind and body.

Types of Meditation

There are three main types of meditation:

1. Meditation that uses **concentration** to focus the mind. This would include most guided meditations, visualization techniques, Silva meditation methods, the use of mantras (such as transcendental meditation), focusing on the breath or counting backward.

2. Mindfulness or **awareness meditation** methods are used extensively in Zen and many other schools of Buddhism. The goal of this type of meditation is to be fully aware of what is happening in the moment,

with all senses engaged.

3. Just **Being**. This type of meditation is also known as "Just Sitting," "Shikan Taza" in Japanese, or "Dzog Chen" in Tibetan. This is the simplest, most advanced and most difficult form of meditation, for which there are no instructions.

Body Posture

Traditionally with eastern forms of meditation, students sit on a cushion in a lotus or cross-legged position with a straight spine. Using a cushion to elevate your rear allows you to form a tripod with your knees and buttocks for maximum stability.

Full or half lotus are the most stable positions for meditation, but if you are like most people, that may not be comfortable or even possible for you. If that is the case, sit in a chair.

The most important aspect of meditation posture is a **straight spine** with your diaphragm muscles slightly stretched, to facilitate the flow of breath.

For relaxing and quieting your mind, any comfortable sitting position where your spine is straight is acceptable. If you have a health problem that makes sitting physically challenging for you, you can lie on your back.

General Instructions

1. Before meditating, decide on the length and method of the meditation practice. Make sure you are in a quiet place with your phone set on airplane mode. You can set a timer with a gentle gong to alert you when the practice period is over.

2. The biggest misunderstanding people have about meditation is the idea that it requires you not to think. Good luck with that! Thinking is natural. We all do it all the time.

3. The goal of concentration in meditation is to FOCUS your thinking—not stop it. It is natural, especially in the beginning, for your mind to wander. If it does, simply bring your mind back.

Concentration Meditation Techniques

There are many forms of concentration meditation. When people are stressed or anxious, they are typically focused on past events or worst-case scenarios about what could happen in the future. When you refocus your mind with concentration or visualization techniques, you can experience relief immediately. The more inner senses you engage, the more likely you will be to stay focused for longer periods. Here are some options:

1. Use a guided audio (MindToSucceed.com).

2. Count backward from 100 to 1. You may want to imagine writing the numbers on a whiteboard, or in the sand on the beach, or some other way that holds your attention.

3. Focus on a candle, flower or object.

4. Focus on repeating a mantra or affirmation to yourself.

5. Imagine a scene that you find relaxing and enjoyable. Use all your senses, imagine the sights, sounds, smells, feelings, etc.

6. Use progressive relaxation techniques, starting at the top of your head and working your way down to your toes, consciously relaxing each part of your body as you go. If you prefer, start at your toes and work your way up to the crown of your head.

7. Concentrate on an idea, inquiry or Zen Koan.

Mindful Meditation Techniques

This type of practice focuses on awareness of what is happening in the moment. The goal of mindful meditation is to stay present and aware of what is happening right now.

As a sitting practice, mindful meditation is about turning your attention inward. But you can also practice mindfulness with eyes open, while eating, walking, doing yoga or repetitive tasks. The goal is to stay present, observing your senses and whatever else arises. It sounds easy, but you may be surprised.

Tips for Meditating

1. Get into a habit of setting time aside each day when you won't be interrupted.
2. You are not striving for anything, so just relax. It is natural sometimes to feel resistance. When you do, cultivate a healthy curiosity around what is going on and meditate around the places you feel stuck.
3. Use your breath as an anchor to keep coming back to throughout the practice period.
4. If you find your mind wandering repeat a suggestion on every third exhale such as "deep stillness."
5. Be kind to yourself. If you get carried away by your thoughts, immediately forgive yourself and come back to concentrating on your breath again. Do this no matter how many times it happens. You are human.

Pain Relief

The key to this exercise is to surrender to, not resist, the pain you are feeling. Relaxation is key, and when you resist, you naturally become tense.

1. Begin by focusing on your breath, taking nice slow deep breaths and exhaling slowly. Maintain a rhythmic flow of breath throughout the exercise. If you get distracted, come back to your breath.
2. Scan your body and accept whatever it is you are feeling without resistance.
3. Breathe into the area where you feel the most amount of discomfort for a few moments until you feel yourself relaxing and opening.
4. Visualize rich, oxygenated blood flowing into that area, bringing nourishment and healing. Keep breathing slowly and deeply.
5. Imagine a pain meter in front of a big dial marked in fives from 0 to 100. Notice where the discomfort is on the dial, and imagine it diminishing as you count backward in fives.
6. See the dial going down to zero and imagine how it

feels with the discomfort dial at 0: healed, healthy, free of suffering.

7. Don't look for the pain. Imagine yourself feeling well and vibrant. Tell yourself that you are feeling better and better.

Resourceful State

To bring on a resourceful state such as courage, confidence or clarity:

1. Identify the state that would be most helpful to you now.
2. Remember a time when you felt the way you want to feel now.
3. Imagine stepping into *That You*. Notice, in as much detail as you possibly can, what happened right before you felt that way, what you saw, what you heard, what you felt.
4. Live the experience as if it is happening now. See it. Hear it. Feel it. Carry the feeling with you into the present and notice what is different.
5. If this is a resource you need for something in the future, imagine stepping into that situation with this resource available to you, noticing what is different now.
6. If you want to have this resource consistently available to you in the future:
   - Imagine stepping into a future possible

situation where previously the resource was not easily accessible to you. Play out the situation in your mind, having full access to it, and notice what is different.

- Think of another possible future situation where this resource could help you. Play out the scene and notice what is different now that you have this resource easily accessible. Repeat this step five times with different scenarios.

Tonglen Practice

Tonglen is a mindful practice of letting go of negative feelings. Literally, the Tibetan word means "sending and taking." More than a meditation practice, it is an attitude, a truly beautiful way of transmuting the pain of our lives into a sense of being connected to others.

Part 1:

1. When you feel suffering, breathe it in with the intention to completely feel it, accepting it, and owning it.
2. When you breathe out, send yourself a wish of healing, compassion, loving-
3. kindness or whatever you feel you need in that moment.
4. Repeat the above steps for a few minutes to encourage a feeling of relaxation and openness.

Part 2:

5. Add people you know into the mix who've also experienced the type of pain you are feeling by breathing in and acknowledging the suffering you share.
6. Breathe out, sending a wish that they too be freed from this suffering.
7. Repeat steps five and six for a few minutes.

Part 3

8. Think of all the people in the world who currently share in this experience of anger, grief, anxiety, depression or pain—or whatever it is that you are working with. Breathe in, acknowledging your common suffering.
9. Breathe out kindness, compassion and/or whatever you feel is called for with the wish that you all be relieved of this suffering.
10. Think of all the people who have come before you and all the people who will come after you who will share the experience of whatever it is that you are working with.
11. Breathe in, acknowledging your common suffering. Send out a wish or prayer that you all be relieved of this suffering. Repeat this step for a few minutes.

Trauma Technique

This NLP technique was originally developed by Richard Bandler to desensitize traumatic events. However, it can also be used to eliminate the negative emotional charge of irrational thoughts or fears.

It is never advisable to get rid of a fear when you could be in danger. For example, you wouldn't want to get rid of a fear of walking into a street with high-speed oncoming traffic.

For traumatic events or phobias, this technique should only be used only under the guidance of a trained, licensed professional.

The first time you learn a new technique, begin practicing with small issues and build your way up to bigger things. That strategy will give your mind the opportunity to learn the technique without also having to cope with unnecessary anxiety. Stress and anxiety negatively affect brain functioning and learning ability.

1. Select a fear, recurring thought or traumatic memory you want to desensitize.
2. On a 0-10 scale (0 = Peace, 10 = Trauma) how

traumatic is this memory?

3. Would it be okay to neutralize this? (You must get to "yes" before proceeding. In other words, it rationally makes sense—because you are no longer in danger from this threat.)

4. Get into a neutral or good state before you continue with the process (not where you were in the measuring of step 2.) You can get up and dance, stretch, go to your peaceful place—whatever you need to be calm and resourceful.

5. Imagine what the back of your head would look like if you saw yourself sitting a few feet in front of where you are now. Imagine seeing the back of your head. Your eyes can be open or closed, whatever makes it easier for you to visualize.

6. Now imagine that *That You, who is sitting in front of you,* has a black and white video of the younger you who had the experience you are working with. (It is *That You* who has the video, who is going to do the rest of the work. This is important because you want to remove yourself from the experience so that you don't get triggered during this work.) This video starts at a neutral or happy place, before the younger person had that bad experience, and ends at a neutral or happy point, after the bad thing happened and that person survived it.

7. Across the room, high up, in front of the *That You* who has the video, is a small TV with a video player

that can only play at very fast speed. The TV is on and all you see is static fuzz.

8. *That You* who has the video will put the video in, and you will see a freeze frame BEFORE the bad scene when everything was neutral or happy. Then *That You* will press the play button on the remote he or she is holding, and it will play_**very fast**_through the bad experience to the end where the neutral or happy scene is, after *That You* survived that situation. The entire video plays from beginning to end in less than two seconds. BRRRROOOOMM. You will watch *That You* watching the video, and at the end of the video, static fuzz will appear on the screen.

9. Now let *That You* put the video in where it is freeze-framed on the neutral/happy scene. Remember that you are watching *That You* who is watching the video. Now watch *That You* push the play button and the entire video plays in one and a half seconds. BRRROOOOMM. Static fuzz plays on the TV screen.

10. Now watch as *That You* rewinds the video and it plays backwards to the beginning scene in one and a half seconds. BRRROOOOMM. Static on the TV.

11. Repeat several times.

12. Watch as *That You* turns the video and TV upside down, so that the movie will play upside down, so that people's heads are toward the bottom and their feet are on top—as if they are standing on their heads.

Now watch *That You* play the whole video upside down in one and a half seconds. BRRROOOOMM. There is only static on the TV now.

13. Now *That You* plays it backwards upside down. BRRROOOOMM. Now fast forward upside down. BRRROOOOMM. Now fast reverse back to the happy/neutral time. BRRROOOOMM. Fast forward BRRROOOOMM. Fast reverse. BRRROOOOMM. The neutral/happy time is on the screen.

14. *That You* takes the video out and discards it.

15. Check your feelings of the event now (0 = Peace, 10 = Trauma) If your feelings are not all the way down to zero, repeat the process, asking your unconscious mind to take care of whatever was missed the first time.

For more self-help exercises and audio guides, please visit MindToSucceed.com.